ON
THE
OUTSIDE
LOOKING
IN

My life on the Autism Spectrum

RUSSELL'S FIRST BOOK "INSIDE OUT" RESONATES WITH READERS

"A compelling story of coming-of-age with autism."

~Los Angeles Times, December 2011

"An emotional and inspiring book that will benefit any-one with autism and their families."

~Reno Gazette Journal, February 2012

2013 Literary Excellence Recipient International Naturally Autistic People Awards Vancouver, Canada

2012 Honorary Mention New York Book Festival

Lisa,

Enjoy, it was a pleasure to meet you.

ON THE OUTSIDE LOOKING IN

My Life on the Autism Spectrum

RUSSELL LEHMANN

A Lucky Bat Book
LuckyBatBooks.com

On The Outside Looking In
My Life on the Autism Spectrum

To order additional copies of this book,
or to book Russell for an event, please visit:
TheAutisticPoet.com

or

Russell-Lehmann.com

1 2 3 4 5 6 7 8 9 10

ISBN 978-1-61475-826-6

Dedicated to my mom.

This book is dedicated to the most important figure in my life, a huge reason behind why I am *WHERE* I am today, and why I am *WHO* I am today. My mom.

My shelter during the toughest of storms, this woman has been the one steady constant in my life. Every single day she is there for me, and whenever I'm on the verge of collapsing, I find refuge in her absolutely unconditional love. Whether I'm succeeding or failing, happy or sad, functioning or not, her love and support is limitless, which in turn makes my own potential limitless.

From her love and affection, I learned to never be ashamed of who I am. From her words of wisdom, I found out that there was a reason behind why I was here. From her ability to listen, I found my voice, and from her just *BEING* there for me, she helped me to see the beauty during the darkest of days, and to always, *ALWAYS* remain positive.

She believed in me when no one else did. She fought for me when I was too weak to fight for myself. She sat next to me during times when I felt completely alone. And she loved me when I was too bitter and angry to love myself.

She is my idol, my mentor, my role model, my hero. But most importantly, I am lucky enough to call this wonderful individual my mother.

Acknowledgements

I would like to thank Nevada Governor Brian Sandoval and Reno Mayor Hillary Schieve for their tremendous support these past two years and for being kind enough to write the introductions to this book.

Also deserving of many thanks is my team at Lucky Bat Books. Layout designer Holli McCarty and publisher Cindie Geddes.

Lastly, I have to thank all my supporters, fans and every member of every audience I have had the privilege of presenting in front of. You all give me something to hold onto during my dark moments, and make the fire within me to spread awareness, acceptance and compassion burn brighter and hotter.

Be you. Be Original.

"Never, never, never quit"

~Winston Churchill

Contents

Contents

Contents

Contents

Foreword

Finding your voice.

It's such a simple concept, yet it can be a lifelong challenge. It's discovering and unlocking our potential in the midst of obstacles from outside and within.

And for me, Russell Lehmann is one of the finest examples of how we can find our voices in courage.

Russell has turned his challenges into a message and movement for thousands of others. Finding his own voice has helped create influence and agency for so many of others on the spectrum and the people who love them. That comes from looking at those challenges as strengths.

He calls his life with autism "a gift that's just really hard to open." Sometimes in life those shifts in perspective help. Russell has been in deep and dark places. Some far more harrowing than others. He's talked about the struggle of feeling unwanted and isolated in public. We can't "see" autism like other hurdle keeps these challenges hidden in a way most of us don't understand.

Russell finds that hidden truth within himself and brings it to the surface. He often talks about his goal and his message. He wants us to dream. It's a potent idea coming from a man who easily could have let life and his struggles break down hope.

Medical setbacks are often out of our control. They are handed to us without warning or reason or justification. A diagnosis can feel like the weight of bricks on our shoulders and a torment we can't escape. At times we're powerless as we watch the people we love battle with themselves.

Yet through all of that, Russell tells us that the strength to get through the darkness comes from letting go of fear. It's recognition and awareness that our challenges don't define us. They can't force us into one life over another.

He's found his voice and Russell continues to be an inspiration to us all. Thank you for being a special part of Reno, with a special place in my heart.

~Mayor Hillary Schieve
Reno, Nevada
2019

Introduction

This is not your typical book.

Most books with personal stories and poems will mix the two into one big story. But after many long conversations, my publisher and I decided to do something different. Actually, several somethings different.

As you will see as you peruse the pages of this book, I am utterly and unapologetically raw and transparent. I am human, I am not indestructible and I am by no means perfect. I thought it proper to also recognize the faults in this book.

Having said this, you will see various errors, typos other oddities. This, I chose to do on purpose.

The human condition is one of the lessons learned from our greatest struggles. I thought it apropos to exemplify this in the pages of a book that is an intimate insight into my vulnerabilities, naiveties and painful, traumatic experiences.

I am who I am, and I strive to be a better human each and every day. Personal growth is only possible when we recognize and accept the faults about ourselves.

ON THE OUTSIDE LOOKING IN

We have arranged this book to be representative of how I think. The stories I tell, while emotional and vulnerable, are different from my poetry. My poetry is all emotion. Poetry is what I do when my emotions start to get overwhelming. It is a release and a confession and a love letter and, through it, I tell my story in a completely different way from my life in prose. For that reason, we chose different fonts for memoir versus poetry, and we chose to keep the bulk of the poetry in one section and the personal stories in their own section. That said, there are a few points in my life where a poem is such an organic part of the experience that we decided to keep the poem in both the memoir and the poetry sections.

Between the memoir and the poetry sections are some pages that summarize some of the big lessons I've learned. This section belongs with neither the memoir nor the poetry section. Both the memoir and the poetry sections lead to this center. This is where I have ended up. I acknowledge the help I've received and leave you with some lessons I've learned. The center section is the culmination of what has happened to me and how I've felt about it. Leaving the middle section to stand on its own reflects where I am now, able to stand up, tell my whole story and leave you with some thoughts to remember. Poetry and memoir, together, lead to the point where I can use my trauma to help others understand autism better AND get through their own lives just a little bit more easily. And that is my goal, not only with the book but with my life.

The journey of publishing has been eye-opening. It took several tries before we felt like we'd captured my personality. The designer would lay out the book, only to find it didn't guide the reader to where I am now the way we wanted it to. The poetry pulled people out of the story. And the story watered down the poetry. But when we decided to separate them and change the fonts, the whole project clicked.

The science backs up why this worked. What happens in your brain when you read poetry is different from what happens when you read prose. Scientists have even been able to map the reactions. The part of your brain that lights up when you read poetry is completely separate from the part that lights up during reading of prose. Scientists have shown that poetry excites emotion in a way prose doesn't. So what better way to experience a book with poetry and prose than to separate them the same way the brain does? When you read the memoir section, we want you committed to coming along for the ride. When you get lit up by poetry, we want to keep you lit up. We want you to feel the emotional ups and downs, just like I did going through it all.

My first book, which was published in 2011, Inside Out: Stories and Poems from an Autistic Mind, opened with the following lines: "Closed on the outside, open on the inside.

ON THE OUTSIDE LOOKING IN

That's how I would describe myself living with autism. Throughout my whole life I have walked the long, lonely roads and have struggled to come out of many valleys. I have also had some triumphs, and poetry is one of them."

Since the publication of this first book of mine, I have continued to find myself lost in many dark valleys, however I have also scaled the highest of peaks. I have not had "some triumphs," as stated above, but rather I have triumphed. Over my struggles, disorders, hardships and external circumstances.

My name is Russell Lehmann, and I am an internationally recognized and award-winning motivational speaker, poet, author and advocate. Oh, and I just happen to have autism.

My life has been one long, treacherous road, until recently, when I was able to brush aside the overgrown hedges to reveal the beautiful sunshine that I had been walking toward my whole life.

How did I get here? Courage. Tenacity. Perseverance. Love. Support. I learned through trial and error to not let my emotions dictate my actions, and, most importantly, I learned that I would never get anywhere in life unless I could truly believe in myself.

A few years ago, I made a promise to myself that all the pain, anguish and agony that I have encountered would not be in vain. I made a commitment to use my experiences, and the lessons that I have learned from them, to help others overcome their challenges. I am here to give others support, inspiration and hope. I'm here to show the world that I can overcome any challenge that comes my way, and that every obstacle that confronts me, is just another chance for me to attain knowledge and personal growth.

Above all, I am here to show the world that I embrace my challenges, and that we should all embrace our challenges. Yes, they make us who we are, but they do so much more than that. They inspire hope, change, accomplishment and, yes, belief. Our challenges inspire belief. This one thing that we all need in order to attain our goals, we receive when we embrace the challenges we are dealt.

I have been there; I have suffered. I have done that; I have struggled. I take solace in believing that since I have been through a vast array of agonizing scenarios in my life, sharing my story and insights will spare others from having to encounter any unnecessary pain in their lives. There is far too much needless, redundant pain and sorrow in this world.

It is my hope that reading this book will unveil to you the beauty of personal struggles. The magnificence of hardships. The splendor of battling your demons.

Before we begin, I would like to introduce you to a little boy. This little boy was pretty much nonverbal. He was too afraid of the outside world to speak to anyone other than his parents. When he did talk, he had such a severe speech impediment that only his mother and father could understand what he was saying. He stayed inside his house whenever he could, clinging to his parents' sides, terrified of any external stimuli, such as the doorbell ringing, the TV being on, or the microwave going off. He once mentioned that he felt as if he were a prisoner inside his own body. During this time in his life he was extremely low-functioning and could barely take care of himself.

He was the only kid who cried during the first day of school, and any friends that he managed to make were lost once he started to become reclusive. To fill the deep, dark void of soon having no contact with the outside world, this little boy would form friendships with inanimate objects such as slices of pizza, furniture and balls. He would give these objects names and even sleep with them in his bed. If an object that this young boy had an attachment to was thrown away, damaged or lost, this boy would suffer from debilitating anxiety and depression, sobbing as he paced back and forth across the room, sometimes for hours, as he mourned the loss or injury of a true friend.

This little boy was so kind-hearted and innocent, yet his life seemed to be a living hell. At his worst, he would experience both auditory and visual hallucinations; at his best he mustered up just enough energy to make it out of bed in the morning, only to go back to bed 15 minutes later. This young boy would also have olfactory hallucinations, smelling people and food he saw on TV, as well as people he saw walking by his bedroom window. All these foreign and oftentimes horrid smells would greatly frighten him, usually leading to an hour-long meltdown. He had many severe phobias such as germs, open spaces, bugs, people, etc., all of which slowly destroyed his life and incapacitated him when he came into contact with them. He would wash his hands until they became so dry they would bleed, experience a meltdown if he came within eyesight of a bug and have a panic attack if he was not in the immediate vicinity of his mother.

I happened to be a witness to these panic attacks and meltdowns, and let me tell you, they were not pretty. This boy would rock back and forth violently in an effort to help soothe the absolutely debilitating agony he was experiencing, but all in vain. His limbs and neck would twitch, his jaw slowly clenching his tongue in an attempt to distract himself from the mental pain and utter confusion, but again, this was just a wasted effort. The crying, moaning echoes of torment and anguish would bounce off the walls of the room he was in, the sound alone enough to bring his parents to tears. His breathing would periodically stop due to mental and emotional exhaustion, his body's basic functions failing to keep up with what his brain demanded.

He would punch, hit and slap himself all over his body, especially his head. This boy was insightful enough, however, to know that he should only hurt himself in places that wouldn't be visible to others. He would punch holes in walls and throw the nearest object with all his might, all the while destroying himself on the inside with the guilt he felt from doing all of this in front of his mother. Every time this young boy would have a meltdown in front of his mom--this woman whom he loved more than anything in the universe--he died a little on the inside, and who knows if that part of him ever came back to life.

During these crises, the boy's fingers would be chewed into nubs. Almost nothing was left of his nails, and he would dig so deep into his skin that each finger would be bleeding profusely. Again, anything to escape the mental misery.

These meltdowns would last for hours, and afterward this young boy would fall slowly into a deep sleep. He once told me that during the times he would fall asleep after an arduous battle with his brain, he felt as if death was overcoming him. A slow, comforting, soothing death. Lying in bed with all of his emotions slowly but steadily dissipating, he was incapable of feeling anything other than numbness. He could not think coherently and was unable to comprehend even the simplest words said to him. His muscles, beginning in his legs, would slowly stop twitching, the gentle, soothing sensation of stillness slowly creeping its way up into his arms and then finally his neck. His breathing was fully functional again, deep breaths in and out, his sternum softly shaking, recovering from the trauma his body had recently endured. The blood from his fingers would finally stop flowing, and this little boy's eyes would slowly blink, eventually staying closed as he drifted off into a deep, much needed rest.

I hear this little boy, who is now a grown man, still suffers from these episodes today.

This boy? He is me.

My intentions for this book are to help those struggling with anything in life, whether that be a disability or simply an external circumstance, know that they are not alone and to let them know that there is indeed light at the end of the tunnel, they just have to believe it. When we are pushed into a corner with seemingly no way out, will we give up or get up? Shall we succumb or overcome? The choice is up to us!

The poems featured in this book cover a wide array of topics. However, a lot of them are very personal and they will hopefully give you an insight into the personal experiences I encounter on a daily basis and how I managed to not only conquer my demons, but to enslave them and make them work for me instead of against me.

The following is my story, and it is my sincere hope that you walk away with insight and inspiration, hope and fearlessness.

Enjoy.

ON THE OUTSIDE LOOKING IN

1990–1995

I was born on December 5, 1990. My parents were extremely excited because they'd had three miscarriages before me. However, the day turned out to be pretty terrifying for them. When I was born, my entire body was dark blue due to lack of oxygen. I was also, in the doctor's words, "very floppy" (which is a little-known early sign of autism), meaning that I had poor muscle tone for a baby. He said that this was also due to lack of oxygen. Luckily, once he gave me oxygen, I responded right away. The blue drained from my body, and my skin color started to look normal.

During the first couple of months of my life, I slept much more than the average baby. I also did not move my arms very much and had slightly delayed motor skills. I did not learn to sit up until I was nine months old, the average being five months. However, the doctors thought nothing of it and said it was just because I was a big baby (I was born 9 lb. 3 oz.). By the time I was two years old, I was still not talking at all. If I wanted something, I would just point and grunt. Finally, after three long years, I started to make progress with my speech.

When I was three, I started experiencing episodes where I would black out, sometimes due to over stimulation, sometimes just out of the blue with seemingly no reason whatsoever. The very first time I had a blackout occurred when my grandpa was visiting. My mom and he were talking at the kitchen table, and I was right outside sitting on a bench eating a yogurt. All of a sudden, through the window, my mom saw all the color drain from my face, and I immediately slouched over, totally out cold.

My mom immediately rushed out and put her hands on my shoulders in order to hold me up. It took a good amount of time, but I eventually came around. When I was fully conscious again, I got up right away, and for the rest of the day, I acted perfectly normal, with no memory of what had happened.

The next time I had a blackout episode was when my uncle came to visit. I opened the front door as he arrived and ran outside, fully functional. Not twenty seconds later, however, I dropped to the ground, once again losing all consciousness. My mom, dad, and uncle ran over to me and saw that I was dark blue. It didn't take long for me to wake up this time, but when I did, I started crying. Later that week, my mom and I were standing in our driveway when, once again, she saw all the color drain away. She knew what to expect this time, so she was able to catch me as I dropped to the ground.

This time, I did not lose consciousness, but I was very dazed and confused. My parents immediately called the doctor on call (it was the weekend), and he met us at the hospital. He scheduled numerous tests to be done later that week, including an EEG (electroencephalography). When my parents finally received the results, nothing abnormal showed up. They didn't know whether to be scared or happy. Throughout the next ten months, I kept having these episodes. My parents were able to learn the signs when I was about to collapse: I would completely freeze and stop breathing. They would tell me, in a loud voice, to breathe and would gently shake me. At once, I would slowly start to breathe again, subsequently acting as if nothing had happened. My very last blackout was at the age of 5, and I never again experienced an episode like this. We never did find a reason behind why these instances occurred.

1997

Throughout the ages of six to ten, my mother would work the night shift at Children's Hospital in Seattle as a respiratory therapist every Sunday. I dreaded these nights, for as a little boy I never felt safer than when I was at my mother's side, and the sadness and despair I felt from having to go to bed without kissing her good night tore me apart. The following is a brief written account of these nights I wrote for a college class back in 2011.

Through the Storm Comes Love

The last day of the weekend never did treat me well. It was an early winter night and the darkness started to prevail. A storm was brewing, not just in the sky, but in my mind. It was 7 p.m. and my mother was getting ready to leave for work. As a respiratory therapist, her job was to help save people's lives. My life, however, felt far from saved once she walked out the front door. I was a young boy, not yet ten, who suffered from severe separation anxiety. Every Sunday night, my mother was scheduled to work the night shift at Children's Hospital in Seattle, and one week never went by without me pleading for her to stay home. The pain was immense. Twin rivers would flow down my cheeks, and, merging at my chin, would empty into my heart, the ocean of my pain. How could this winter night become ever darker?

The time had finally come for my mother to leave. She gave me a kiss, bent down, and told me not to worry. As she hesitantly closed the door (for I am sure she did so with much pain), it was as if I became possessed by a tornado. Flying up the stairs, the salty rain began to pour. I would rush into my bedroom closet and slam the door; the thunder had begun. My father (you could call him a storm-chaser, I suppose) remained calm and waited for the rain to stop. Once it did, he opened the doors to my closet. I knew what he was going to say, yet in some obscure fashion, I did not know what I was going to hear. "Think you're ready to go get some ice cream now?" At last, the storm was beginning to pass.

As my father drove us down to our local ice cream shop, the skies had started to clear. The shimmer of the moon gleamed down upon the building with such grace, almost as if it was guiding us toward happiness, or, should I say refuge, if perhaps the storm were to come back. Once inside, I felt like a kid in a candy store, only this time it wasn't candy, but ice cream. It took me not five seconds to decide what I was going to get. Without hesitation, I told my father that I wanted the vanilla ice cream with chunks of Reese's peanut butter cups. However, I didn't need to tell him that, for he already knew that speaking up for myself was the main part of my recovery effort.

This storm continued to roll in every Sunday for many years, throughout which the same outline of events routinely unfolded. This wasn't a matter of luck or even persistence on my part, but a feeling of unity so tightly bound through love of family. Of course, I only gained this insight a few years after the storm had, at long last, cleared.

To think back on this whole experience from a much-matured outlook, I can see the lessons I learned. For one, I know now that love and acceptance from a family cannot be expected. A force of nature, such as a storm, puts to the test not only the strength of those affected, but of those who surround the affected. However, you needn't take my word for it. Life has a tendency to force us each to discover the lessons we need on our own.

Through hardships come perseverance, through adversity comes strength, and through storms comes love. This, my friends, is surely the greatest gift of all.

2000

In March of the year 2000, I came down with a severe case of bronchitis. I was not able to attend school for two weeks, and I ultimately became so comfortable staying cooped up in the safety of my home that when I had recovered, I didn't want to go back to school. There was so much anxiety building up inside me that even thinking about leaving my house was terrifying. This was my first major encounter with the absolutely debilitating monster that is severe social anxiety.

I sucked my thumb up until the age of 14 as a coping mechanism, and I soon developed a severe speech impediment from doing so. Who would have thought that one day I would be an articulate man who travels the country giving public speeches?

ON THE OUTSIDE LOOKING IN

My mom was relentless in always trying to support me in order to help me maintain some level of normalcy in my life. She would always try to help me muster up the courage to walk down to the bus stop, but I could never do it, I just didn't have it in me. This was perhaps the first time in my life where I felt dead on the inside, a precursor to the devastating depression that would become my lifelong nemesis.

There were some occasions where I was able to start walking to the bus stop, but once I started to draw closer and saw all my friends, I made a beeline for home, tears of fear flowing down my cheeks. I was falling victim to another new demon that had suddenly entered my life: agoraphobia.

After a good week of repeating this effort which was ultimately deemed futile, my mother thought of a different approach. She'd have me get ready for school in the morning, and then she would drive me down to school in our car. I was very excited and optimistic about this plan. Even though I was scared to go near them, I missed my friends with all my heart. I would wake up in the morning feeling confident that I could overcome this endeavor. However, when the time came to get in the car to leave, my mind went into overdrive. I was hit with major panic attacks and would drop to the floor and curl up in a ball. My mom, who suffered from anxiety herself, and per the advice of my doctor, thought that if I worked through this and was able to take that first step into the classroom, I would start to calm down and begin to go with the flow. Now this may have worked if I was only suffering from anxiety, but little did we know back then, in the early stages of what would turn out to be my lifelong struggles, that this was not the case with me.

Each day that passed turned out to be another unsuccessful attempt at aiding me to attend school. My well-being was deteriorating day by day, and no longer did I have the strength nor motivation to keep trying to go to school, but this is exactly what I did, I kept trying. During this prolonged string of unsuccessful attempts to maintain whatever was left of my previously normal routine, I began to experience meltdowns for the very first time in my life, curling into a ball on the floor, sobbing incoherently. Yet, every morning, after crying for what seemed like hours, I was somehow able to stand up and walk to the garage door, making another attempt to get in the car and have my mother drive me to school. We would never make it more than halfway to school, when I would break down once again and beg my mother to turn around and take me home.

ON THE OUTSIDE LOOKING IN

One day, however, when I was about to walk into the garage in the midst of another fruitless endeavor to just simply go to school, I froze underneath the door frame.

My sole objective was to not take a single step outside of my house. My mom, being extremely stressed out and not knowing what to do, along with the fact that I couldn't miss another day of school, grabbed me around the waist and tried to usher me into the car. With all my might, I grabbed hold of the door frame and hung on for my life. Sobbing and screaming at the top of my lungs, my mom, who was crying herself, pulled and pulled, but I would just not let go. She finally gave up, knowing that all she was doing was making it worse. I was allowed to go back into the house, and I ran straight up to my room and hid in my bed. This scene repeated itself for the next week, with me gradually making as much progress as to be driven down to the school. But once again, when it was time for me to get out of the car, I shut down into panic mode.

My mom tried to comfort me and told me that she would walk to my class with me, but it was no use. Once again, per the instructions of my doctor, she tried pulling me out of the car. And once again, I hung on to the car door, refusing to let go. Of course, I was also sobbing and screaming again. But my mom knew better. She never wanted to make me feel worse, and I can't even imagine how she felt trying to force me out of the car. She discarded the doctor's advice, knowing that what she was doing was making the situation extraordinarily worse. She drove me home and called the school for the twentieth time in as many school days to let them know that I was not going to be able to make it in.

I ended up staying home for three and a half months. My mom would pick up schoolwork for me to do at home, but I was in such a bad shape that I was not able to function mentally.

After numerous accommodations being demanded from my teacher by my parents, I was finally able to go back to school, but that first day back was beyond excruciatingly terrifying. My biggest phobia was being bombarded with all my friends' questions as to why I stopped going to school. I was one of the most popular kids, so I knew that every single kid was going to ask me something. All I could say to them was "I don't know" or "Because." At this point in my life, I started wearing a hoodie over my head whenever I went out in public, especially when I went to school, in order to feel as secure and safe as possible.

In April, I had a severe allergic reaction to one of my medications. I was very happy that evening because we were eating my favorite meal—macaroni and cheese. During dinner, however, my throat began to swell shut. I couldn't eat, and it was extremely hard for me to breathe and swallow. This theme always seemed to constantly occur during this treacherous period of my life. Once something good is going for me or when I am just simply happy, everything starts to turn for the worse. This was one of those times.

That night was definitely one of the scariest moments in my life. I was crying so much and kept asking my mom if I was going to die. I can't imagine how that made her feel, a mother's own child scared he was going to die. This is one of the worst things about having autism that many people do not know. It killed me on the inside to be going through such pain while at the same time also knowing that I was possibly destroying my own family's lives.

My parents had to call 911, and an ambulance was rushed over to our house. I can still remember our neighbors looking through their window as I was lifted into the ambulance. I wondered why I couldn't be on the other side of that window. I ended up spending four hours in the ER. The doctors gave me a breathing treatment with epinephrine, and my throat finally started to open up. My family and I were all extremely relieved. I never thought that breathing could be so enjoyable.

About two days later, my family and I went on a vacation to Europe. Although the timing for this trip could not have been worse with regards to what was occurring in my life, my father had booked this vacation years in advance. We decided as a family that even though I was barely able to function, we would attempt to make the most out of the trip. I was, in fact, looking forward to this trip since the day my father booked it.

Unfortunately, this two-week trip would turn out to be pure hell. The very first day we were there, I started to feel uncomfortable. We had landed in Charles de Gaulle Airport in Paris, France, and I could already tell how different their culture was. I'm sure some of it was just my imagination, but people looked, dressed and smelled totally differently, which scared me. Throughout this two-week trip, we also visited Switzerland and Germany. There were a lot of fun times; however, the rest of the time I was totally out of control due to being extremely anxious and overwhelmed.

Our whole family was torn apart during this vacation. We were constantly at one another's throats and everyone was very upset with me because they still didn't fully understand what I was going through. After all, these negative symptoms in my life were still somewhat new to all of us, even me. I refused to eat anything, not even American food like McDonald's or simple sandwiches. I ended up having several severe panic attacks and extreme bouts of depression, and each day my OCD gained in its strength. I cannot even try to explain the mental anguish that I was going through. I was only nine years old and had already lived through a lifetime of problems.

After two weeks passed in Europe, we were all very much relieved to be heading back home. My whole family was emotionally and physically exhausted, and I couldn't help but feel like the culprit in this horrendous trip. After all, my symptoms were the catalyst behind all the fights and arguments that took place. However, once we got home, I received the greatest gift when my whole family told me, all at once, that nothing was my fault. They all knew, somewhat surprisingly, that the dysfunction of a family falls on every member's shoulders evenly.

2001

In May of 2001, when I was in fourth grade, summer was approaching very fast. I had seemingly recovered from my phobia of school ever since I was able to begin attending again the previous year after a long absence. Up until this time, I had a great overall school year. However, as the last day of school drew closer and closer, I started to get very overwhelmed with all the commotion that comes at the end of the school year. In addition, my class was planning a field trip to the zoo, and although I was very excited about this, sometimes my excitement gets the best of me.

One morning, about 1 month before the final day of school, seemingly out of the blue, I stopped dead in my tracks as I was about to walk out the front door to the bus stop. I was all of a sudden terrified to leave the house, and

ON THE OUTSIDE LOOKING IN

I cannot describe to you how chilling it was to once again feel the emotions that were behind my inability to attend school the previous year. Of course, I was very worried that these feelings of fear and anxiety were the start of what would turn into that same debacle that happened during the previous school year. Unable to walk out the front door that day, I stayed home, hoping that I was just having a bad day and that the next day would be better.

Unfortunately, my anxiety would not stop growing that day. I already missed my friends and did not want to lose contact with them once again. That was my biggest fear, to be isolated and alone while I was battling my demons all alone, in solitude and silence. I also dreaded the possibility of missing out on the field trip to the zoo.

I ultimately ended up missing two weeks of school due to severe social anxiety, panic attacks, depression and multiple phobias. However, there was a silver lining in all of this. I was finally able to muster up the courage of going back to school, just like I did the year before, but not before the field trip had come and gone. I was able to finish the last 2 weeks of the school year in good spirits and I really believed that the worst of my struggles were behind me. I felt the freedom and joy of being a kid again, and my family and I were extremely proud of the fact that I had finally conquered my demons.

Soon, though, they would come back to conquer me.

2002

One morning in May of 2002, when I was in 5th grade, I had an appointment with my orthodontist to have my braces removed and to be given a retainer to use. I thought nothing of this change beforehand, and after the appointment, my mom drove me to school. It was around 10:30am, and I was scheduled to go into one of my favorite classes: music. I was really looking forward to this class due to the fact that earlier in the week teacher told us we were going to watch a movie and give us popsicles that day. However, once my mother drove me up to the front of the school, that same sensation of dread and doom that I had encountered the previous two years slowly started to roll over my body. I started hyperventilating and crying, which ultimately led to a severe panic attack. I could not get out of the car, I was as frozen as a statue.

After about ten minutes of comforting me and reassuring me that everything would be okay, my mom finally coaxed me out. I was able to take a few steps toward the front doors, which in and of themselves felt like a huge accomplishment, however those few steps would be as far as I could go. I was incapable of walking any farther. Crying, I told my mom that I couldn't do it. She asked me if I was sure, but deep down I know that she already knew the answer. I climbed back into the car and was slowly taken home, my mom driving away hesitantly as she was putting together the all-too-true pieces of a tragic puzzle. My heart sank to my stomach. The beginning of the end was occurring yet again, the time coming for me to say goodbye again to that short-lived essence of an innocent childhood.

As we were leaving the parking lot, I looked back at the school. Although I felt much relief that I was going back to the safety and security of my home, I knew that I had was just starting to play the same game that I had played in third and fourth grade, albeit against an overmatched and unfair opponent. Sadly, unlike the last two games with this demon, this time around I had the feeling that I was not going to win.

This was the last day of my life as I currently knew it. This was the day that ended all my relationships with my friends and, ultimately, led to the complete destruction of my childhood.

This was the day that I stopped living. I was 11 years-old, and I began to only exist, and barely survive.

2003

Cursed to be Normal

I was cursed to be normal, the normality of strange
God must have been drunk when He put together my
brain
I feel like I've been stuck at level 1 of this game
This game of tolerating pain, which I have done
without gain
Problems with me are too much to feel ashamed
Of what has been going on inside of my
brain

Since day 1 x 30 days multiplied by 72 ways

ON THE OUTSIDE LOOKING IN

I have proclaimed I need help, to change my way of
self-esteem
For it has been high everyday
Even though it seems there are no means,
To confiscate the compliments I put away in my dreams

This part of me seems so ugly in the way
That it seems to deem my inner retard everyday
I'm sorry if that offends you in some close-minded way
But just think, this thing inside of me comes out
everyday
Much to my dismay
I feel like I should fly away up to the heavens
And ask God
Why me?

I was 12 when I said I was 13
I wanted to fit in and not lose myself,
Over this OCD
So I sat in C-3, for five straight, strenuous weeks
Until the doctor came and told me
That my treatment was complete
I was free

I was happy at first, but later on that day
I grew angry because the doctor didn't tell me
That there was another school I had to see

RUSSELL LEHMANN

Simple minds and simple times occurred inside that
school
Except for me, for I had my hood up
And drifted off to some tunes
When I was forced into a room of complete solitude
All while knowing that those people, had played me
for a fool
All they ever did, was look for somebody to screw

Mrs. Yappity-Yap and Mr. Do-This-And-Do-That
Were so irritating! They thought they had me in their
laps
But I just blew them off and took three hour naps
Until my mom picked me up, and drove me away from
that trap
I would look back and pray that I wouldn't have to go
back

These ideas stem from a mind
That has been through too much in its time
So calloused it has become, in its long worn out life
From attempts to colonize the insults it has survived
And throw them off to the side

I wish I could give them my life, and see the fear in
their eyes

ON THE OUTSIDE LOOKING IN

As they cry and apologize for the damage they have
done
To a life, so young
And now that life is saying "So long,
You are in the past
For my life has just begun."

Since day one I've been in crisis mode
I cannot even begin to relate
To what a normal life feels like
Until I look it in the face

But still then
I don't see any eyes, ears, nose or mouth
I just see a black hole
That is the epitome
Of what my life is about
But I just keep on staring in the mirror
Trying to figure my life out

My OCD is bittersweet
In the fact that it hurts me and my family
In the fact that it forces me, to always perform
superbly
In the fact that when I go to sleep, I count sheep
infinitely

In the fact that I cannot stop, until I succeed in
everything
Until I'm close to fainting
I train hard because training
Puts a positive reinforcement in me
That I can be anything that I want to be
Say hello to this positive reinforcement, please
His name is OCD
And right now, he is the manipulator that I want him
to be
But then there's a flip side, for he can always turn real
mean
He becomes so very angry, that he thinks the thoughts
in me
And spits out the nasty spews, of his tongue indefinitely
And unfortunately, his tongue is the one I use to speak
So please, somebody help me
For this OCD
Has become the being of existence
That is supposed to be me

In 2003, my anxiety, OCD, phobias and depression and
completely consumed me and taken over my life to the
point that I was admitted to the psychiatric unit at a local
hospital. Although I dreaded being away from home, I

was hopeful about receiving the help that I so desperately needed. We applied for a bed in early January of that year and had to wait four weeks for a bed to become available, as well as to have our application approved. Throughout these weeks I kept picturing what the hospital experience would be like. I thought I would have my own private room with a TV and that my parents would be with me whenever they pleased. I also thought that I would just be interacting with the doctors and no one else. I imagined that my stay at the hospital would be something like a mini-vacation, a break from my recently tortuous routine of isolation, anxiety and obsession, where I would be free to do whatever I want when I was not with the doctors or in therapy. I could not have been more off mark, for the naivety of a 12 year-old has no boundaries.

I was finally admitted to the hospital on February 3rd. I was very reluctant to leave my house that morning, but I persevered because I knew that I needed the help that only inpatient hospitalization could give me. Once my parents and I arrived at the hospital we were taken upstairs to the psychiatric unit where I was to be admitted. My jaw dropped as soon as they opened the doors to the unit. There were kids of all ages, from five to seventeen, running around and being very boisterous, which was extremely overstimulating for me. I instantly became a victim of sensory overload, with the noise being incredibly loud and the abundance of people far surpassing my expectations.

The commotion was so extreme that I felt like I was at a Chuck E. Cheese.

At 12 years old I was hospitalized for five weeks due to severe depression, anxiety and OCD, I was ordered by the doctors at this hospital to attend public school without receiving any support or accomidation from the school.

We were soon ushered into a small room where the admission process took place. After we had filed all of the necessary paperwork, two doctors came in to talk with us. They asked my parents some questions about my background and what their hopes were for admitting me there.

After about twenty-five minutes, one of the counselors came in to show me to my room. I refused to go and started to break down. I didn't think there was any way I could survive in there without either one of my parents.

ON THE OUTSIDE LOOKING IN

The doctors promised me that I would only be away from my parents for just a couple of minutes. I trusted them because I knew that if I didn't, I would not make any progress toward my recovery. I begrudgingly went with the counselor, who introduced me to my roommate. I was definitely in no mood to talk.

Once I entered my room, I stood as still as a statue. Looking out the second-story window and crying, I comforted myself by thinking that my parents would be there any minute. I waited and waited and waited. I never took my eyes off the window, and as the time went by, I grew angrier and angrier. It had been like what seemed forever, and the doctors never even bothered to send someone to give me an update. In the end, I looked out that window, crying my eyes out while never moving once, for just under 4 hours before my parents finally arrived.

I ended up staying in this lock down psychiatric ward for five weeks. Those weeks were, by far, the worst my family and I had ever experienced. There were certain nights when my parents would be able to take me out for an hour or two. One night, my dad came to take me to a movie. Before we left, he gave me three basketball posters for me to put up in my room. I was so excited! I can still remember unrolling them and being in somewhat of a trance. I had been through so much lately that a simple gift like this really cheered me up.

When we arrived at the movie theater, I started to become very anxious. It was a very small, privately owned theater and was, for me anyway, in a gloomy part of Seattle. As we walked inside, I started to have a panic attack, yet I was able to hold myself together as we went and got popcorn and made the walk upstairs into the lone theater. As we sat down, I didn't become more anxious; I became more scared. I was extremely afraid of all the people around us, and being in the dark didn't help either. I told my dad that I couldn't stay there. He was hesitant to get up and asked me if I was sure. I was already crying from having a panic attack, but the guilt I felt was tremendous. Once again, I felt that I was letting my dad down. That evening was supposed to be nothing but fun, a brief escape from the prison that I was in.

We left the theater and walked back to our car. I could tell that my dad was in so much pain from seeing me like this. As we got into the car, he started to break down and cry. I felt like I wanted to die. As we drove away from the theater and back to the hospital, I knew that something bad was going to happen.

We were driving down a hill, and at the bottom, there were cars stopped at a red light. Farther and farther down the hill we went, both of us sobbing in pain. I could see that we weren't slowing down, and we crashed right into the back of the car in front of us. My popcorn flying everywhere, none of us were affected from the crash. We were already way beyond any disturbance a crash could give us. My dad slowly got out of the car, as if in somewhat of a trance, as he began to exchange information with the two women whose car we hit, and to see if they were alright. I remember one of the women coming up to me and asking if I was okay. I just nodded as tears dripped into the remains of the popcorn that I slowly picked at.

I was supposed to be back at the hospital at seven, but I wasn't able to get there until eight thirty. Everything that had happened was starting to sink in, and though somewhat in shock, I walked straight into my room. That night was, by far, one of the worst nights in my life. I can't even put into words the mental destruction that had occurred to me that night. I also will never be able to know what was going through my dad's head that night. To this day, I feel so at fault of what had transpired that torturous night. I was in so much emotional pain that it tore us apart on the inside. I still cannot believe that we were able to stick it out and prevail in the long run.

I did not sleep well that night, and the following morning I had to immerse myself back into the strict routine of the hospital. The main therapy that the doctors provided for me was to confront my fears, a kind of exposure therapy. I had an extremely severe phobia of bugs, the sight of one alone was enough to send me into a meltdown.

One day, my doctor called me into a room. This room was about 15x20 feet, with one window looking out onto the cloudy grounds of the hospital, a lone table and two cold, metal chairs.

Sitting across from the doctor, he asked me how my time at the hospital was going so far, which I shrugged off with an "I don't know" while staring at the floor. Eventually after a few attempts at chit chat, my doctor pulled out a closed metal container from his pocket, gently sliding it in front of me on the table. "Go ahead and open it" he said.

Hesitantly, I followed his directions. As I slowly opened the lid to the container I had no idea what to expect. Was it something good? A reward for sticking out my chaotic time in the hospital? I was still an innocent child, so I really didn't have any expectations that the container would be holding anything bad.

As I finally pulled the lid entirely off to expose what was inside, I froze. The metal container was holding two dead flies. Once I realized that my worst phobia was presented right in front of me, I immediately scooted my chair away from the table. I was in shock. Too distressed to cry, and too afraid to speak, I was as still as a statue.

Usually, whenever I would come into contact with a bug, I would spiral into a brutal combination of a meltdown and panic attack. This time around, however, although I began to feel the emotions of fear and horror, I was unable to process them.

The rest of that session with the doctor is a blur, although when I think back on it, those same exact feelings that I experienced that day come flooding back into my consciousness.

As my time at the hospital progressed, I was met with more encounters with dead bugs. Every day the doctors would present to me anything from dead flies, to dead wasps and bumblebees, all of which were displayed in front of me on that lone table, in that same metal container. The doctors would have me pick them up and examine them. Occasionally, they would go so far as to tell me to put the bugs up close to my face and smell them, all the while not fulfilling their promises to let me leave the room if I were to follow their orders.

I used to look back at this experience of mine with resentment, for it caused me so much pain and stress at the time. However, I've recently come to be thankful for it. Although it may have been too harsh of a treatment to put an already extremely vulnerable child through, it did, in fact help me overcome my phobia of bugs, albeit with new, traumatic memories to carry on my already overburdened shoulders.

The doctors at the hospital would also have me attend a class here and there at my local public school during my stay at the hospital. I had stopped attending my local elementary school the previous year, and was never able to go back. Now, however, my grade had transitioned to a middle school, an environment that I was totally unfamiliar with. With great hesitance, I followed the doctor's orders (although I did not have much say in the matter) and attempted to take part in a middle school class.

When the day had come to attend this class, I was scared to death. Petrified, I sat in a chair in the corner of my hospital room slowly rocking back and forth, with clothes covering every inch of my body aside from my eyes. Tears started to slowly roll down my cheeks as I tried to keep my composure while waiting for the hospital staff to pick me up and drive me to my new middle school.

The staff soon walked into my room, letting me know it was time to go. I felt like the life had been sucked out of me, and, almost like a zombie, I slowly followed the staff to the car, one lifeless step at a time.

Although no major incident, such as a panic attack or meltdown, occurred during my short time in this class, the feeling inside of me was one I'll never forget. I can still feel it now, and I almost cringe at its presence. There is not a name for this feeling, but it's power was immense.

While I was sitting in that classroom, the air was stale, the students' stares cold. A colossal amount of weight felt like it was packed inside of me, while everyone else in the room seemed to be moving around weightlessly. The odor was that of death (how I know this I cannot say) and the sounds in the classroom were that of happiness and normalcy, two states that I thought I would never have the honor of attaining. It was as though the world, and all that I was missing out on, was passing me by right in front of my eyes. I knew deep down that I would never be a functioning student at a public school ever again, and this reality hit me hard as I sat in the corner of this class-room, hood up, head down, clenching a stress ball, with my peers going about their day without a second thought about how lucky they were.

Two worlds so close, yet so far apart.

Luckily I only had to suffer through two of these school visits.

Another exposure therapy that the doctors implement-ed was not allowing my mother and me see each other for extended periods of time, due to my severe separation anxiety from her. There would be times when the hospital staff would literally tear my mother and me apart when she was comforting me during a meltdown.

I do not know who this exercise was harder on, me or my mom.

Throughout these five long weeks in the hospital, the only symptom that had improved was my OCD. My anxi-ety and depression were still sky-high, and the doctors were not able to find an answer as to why I was experiencing so many symptoms.. In the end, the doctors discharged me in order to make room for a new patient. My family and I walked out of that hospital with just as many questions to be answered as we did five weeks prior.

When I arrived home, I began to cry tears of happiness for the first time in my life. I was extremely relieved to be home, however little did I know that the doctors had enrolled me in my public middle school, which I was to attend immediately.

Perceptibly, this attempt at trying to transition me back into public school did not go well, to say the least. The school's attempts to integrate me into the classroom failed miserably as I was not awarded an I.E.P., because I did not yet have a formal diagnosis of autism. In the end, I spent the large majority of my time at school sleeping in the principal's office, due to the fact that I was not at all able to function inside the building, as I would shut down as soon as I entered the school, and was deathly afraid of encountering any people.

I was also bullied when I would come into contact with others, however the sad fact of the matter is that I was bullied more by the teachers and staff than I was the students. They would put me down and yell at me, just because I couldn't function like a typical student.

ON THE OUTSIDE LOOKING IN

After about six months of this, I was finally allowed to complete my schoolwork at home, with the help of a teacher's assistant from the school district.

Shortly after, in late 2003, I was at my pediatrician's office for my annual check-up. My mother was filling my doctor in about everything I had been through, and as my mom relayed to the doctor that we as a family were beginning to grasp at straws, my doctor started to ask questions.

"What does Russell struggle with?" "What are some of his symptoms?" "Has he always had a phobia of school?"

With each of my mom's answers to his questions, my pediatrician began to put together the clues. With vast intrigue and curiosity, my doctor asked my mom perhaps the most important question of my life.

"Have you ever looked into autism?"

My mother was familiar with autism, but never thought twice about it due to the fact that all the medical professionals I saw never brought it up. Until now, that is.

One thing led to another, and soon I was referred to my pediatrician to be tested at the University of Washington's Autism Center, and indeed, this was where I was finally diagnosed with high-functioning autism at the age of 12. This diagnosis was a huge relief and big step forward for my family and me. We felt as a family that we finally had something to work with. We finally knew the cause behind all the turmoil in my life.

The next year, in 2004, my diagnosis was already starting to reap benefits. I was accepted into a specialty school in the Seattle area whose sole purpose was to provide special accommodations to students with special needs. I stayed at this school for 2 years, and the personal growth I experienced while attending this school was astronomical. In those 2 years I went from being completely reclusive and not being able to step one foot inside the classroom, to one of the leaders and role models of the school. The catalyst behind this extensive growth and progress was due to nothing more than taking baby steps.

As Confucius once said, "It doesn't matter how slowly you go, as long as you do not stop".

Aside from my hard work, and pushing myself out of my comfort zone, this progress of mine would not have been possible without the accommodations, acceptance, patience and understanding that I received from the school staff. I was so accustomed to being pushed right into the middle of things and to dive headfirst into any problems I had. That is not how you handle autism, and Overlake knew that.

I cannot overstate how vital and significant support and understanding is to those who are going through dark times. If I were to give all of you just one piece of advice, it would be to accept others for who they are. Do not try to change them, but instead support them in becoming the best version of who they already are, deep down inside.

Support, acceptance and understanding are three things that have the ability to make or break a life.

2006

In the early summer of 2006, I had made so much progress that Overlake suggested I make an attempt to gradually integrate into a mainstream school in September. My family and I felt like I was capable of doing this. Plus, I decided that I wanted to play basketball for my local high school. I had always been in love with basketball, so much that I would spend two to four hours every day playing by myself. It was a great way for me to escape and to just clear my head of any unwanted thoughts that came along with having OCD. I knew that I was good enough to make it to varsity and had envisioned nothing less. So my family, along with the help of Overlake, set up a meeting with my local high school's staff and explained to them my conditions and how we wanted to approach this transition. We decided that I would spend the first half of the day at Overlake and then spend the second half at my high school.

We also met with the school's head basketball coach, Mr. Rumbaugh. We told him that I had autism and that playing basketball was one of my main goals. He seemed pretty open-minded about this and told us how the basketball program works; for example, the tryouts, summer practice, game schedules, etc. He also seemed to understand the fact that playing organized basketball would be extremely beneficial to me. After the two meetings with the school staff and basketball coach, I felt very optimistic leaving the school that morning.

Soon it was already the early summer of 2006. High school basketball practice was about to get underway for the upcoming season, and I was more than ready to shine. I had waited eleven years for this moment. Every day, rain or shine or snow, I would spend two-four hours practicing my game outside of my house. I was absolutely obsessed about improving my skills as a basketball player, and I had tremendous expectations for myself. I was driven, I was hungry, I was ready to change my life for the better by using my extreme devotion to perfect my craft in every which way possible.

I cannot tell you to what extent my devotion to basketball was at during my teenage years. Brooms taped to a ladder? They were my makeshift defenders. 5 pound basketball? To improve my shooting strength.

Dribbling with a blindfold on? To enhance my ball handling skills. Practicing with my right hand taped behind my back? To develop ambidexterity.

I had such a drive to play professional basketball that I would go to the most unusual lengths in order to get ahead. One day, I came across an old book of mine, called Salt in His Shoes. It was a story about Michael Jordan, and part of the book that I never forgot was how he used to put salt in his shoes, hoping that it would make him grow taller. Never being one to follow the crowd, I turned this superstition into my very own, by putting pepper in my shoes instead of salt.

Every night before bed, I would take the pepper shaker up to my room, where I would shake 1/3 of pepper and 2/3 of hope into my basketball shoes. Afterwards I would say a little prayer, and then head off to bed, ecstatic for the morning when I would put my feet into my shoes, and feel the power of the pepper streaming through my bones.

Basketball had always been a great way for me to escape from my life. The exercise would help me to clear my head of any unwanted thoughts that came along with having OCD, while at the same time giving myself something to look forward to, which was unfortunately rare for me. I knew that I was good enough to make my high school varsity team, for every Friday night I would dominate the court at my local gym.

ON THE OUTSIDE LOOKING IN

Throughout the summer of 2006, the high school that I was to transition to held basketball scrimmages that were open to all students two nights a week. I made sure that I never missed a single scrimmage. I had, after all, been looking forward to this moment for over a decade. The first time I attended a scrimmage, I was very nervous. I didn't know any of the kids, and it was a totally different environment than what I was used to. The coach was there, and he introduced me to some of the players, who all seemed pretty nice. An interesting aspect of interacting with the other players was that none of them even knew I had autism, let alone that I was reclusive and hadn't socialized with my peers in years. I assume that to them I was just a very shy kid who really opened up when I had the basketball in my hands.

I started to relax and feel comfortable once I started shooting the ball and moving around. Exercise has always been an extremely important factor in helping me communicate with others. I was able to stay there and play for about an hour and a half. After the scrimmage was over, I was really excited and upbeat because I felt that I had accomplished something pretty impressive. I could not wait to go back again. After all my previous experiences with public schools, I never thought I'd be excited to walk back into a school. As the scrimmages progressed, I felt more and more comfortable every time. Some of the kids had taken a real liking to me even though I barely spoke.

Autism, although it can be a wrecking ball that seems to constantly tear any sort of normalcy out of your life, does in fact have a lot of positive facets to it. One of these aspects that I have always relied heavily upon is the ability to sense people for who they really are. There are many of us on the autism spectrum that are synched up with the energy around us. We have tremendous intuition at times and can simply "feel" if someone does or does not care, has good or bad intentions, is a kind or mean-spirited person, etc.

Looking back, I should've trusted my initial instincts about the basketball coach, because although I wanted to believe that things would work out and that he did truly want to help me in my endeavors, something just began to feel off about him the more I ended up being around him.

As the summer exited its infancy, there were eight more scrimmages lined up on the schedule the coach gave me. Due to my success at integrating with the kids during the previous scrimmages, I was becoming increasingly excited about attending each one. There was one scrimmage to be held each week, and I looked forward to it more than anything else.

I had always had difficulties controlling my Obsessive-Compulsive Disorder and getting ready for the basketball scrimmages were no different. I had developed a meticulous routine to ensure that I would have a great practice and to help calm my nerves. From washing my hands a certain number of times, to making sure my outfit was perfectly even from my head to my toes to tying my shoes hastily, just to be untied and tied again in a more perfect fashion, to stretching every single muscle in my body for at least twenty seconds, my pre-scrimmage routine could take me up to two hours.

After I had finished going through my rituals, my dad would drive me to the high school which was about twenty five minutes away from our house. I remember one time, as my dad drove through the parking lot of the school, that no other cars were there. I was worried that the scrimmage might have been abruptly cancelled, and as my father and I got out of the car and walked into the school, which was unlocked, we saw the coach walking down one of the hallways.

I can still hear the coach's steps echoing throughout the desolate hallway, my heart racing, for I knew that nobody else but the coach was in the school.

My father and I, after what seemed like an eternity, finally caught up to the coach as he continued walking throughout the school. He was very surprised to see us, especially me, as I was dressed in my basketball attire. "There's no scrimmage tonight" he said without us even being able to greet him first. My dad's first reaction was to ask him why not. I was too sad and anxious to even look up from the ground.

"It was cancelled, I thought you knew" the coach said dryly as he started to continue walking down the hallway.

My father and I had to walk briskly to keep up with the coach as he was relentless in continuing to walk. "Here is our phone number, can you please notify us if a practice should ever be cancelled again?" My dad asked. "Yes" was all the coach said as he wandered into a classroom. My father and I decided to stop chasing him.

We headed for the exit, and once we set foot outside the school, I collapsed onto the cold, rough concrete. I was in tears. I was sobbing and moaning and squirming on the ground. I was having a meltdown. My dad tried his best to console me, but there was no use. I had looked forward to this practice all day. All WEEK. It was the only reason I got out of bed that morning. For those of us on the autism spectrum, change is always hard, but unexpected, unfortunate change is the absolute worse. For me anyway, I lose all consciousness of the here and now, and after the intense agony and excruciating mental pain starts to pass, usually after about 30 minutes, I begin to disassociate. All my feelings escape from my body, and I feel numb. I feel nothing. My voice, if I have the energy to talk, is monotone and flat, and I truly don't care about anything during my disassociation.

Eventually I recovered enough to pick myself up off the ground and slowly walk back to the car with my dad. I was devastated. I never wanted to feel this way again, and yet, even after the coach told us he would notify us if the scrimmage was cancelled again, this same exact scene played out three more times that summer.

Needless to say, at this point my parents and I had lost all hope with regards to the coach and him supporting my courageous endeavor.

Soon September arrived; summer had come and gone, and it was time for me to start taking two classes at my high school. The first half of the day was to be spent at Overlake, and the second half at my local high school. I was in tenth grade and was very optimistic about my attempt to attend a mainstream school. I had an individualized education plan (IEP) set up and was confident in my teachers and counselors to provide me with any support I might need. However, they failed to do that on the very first day. When I got to the school, the hallways were crammed with kids, which was extremely overwhelming for me. As fast as I could, I made my way over to my first class, which was English. Anxious to get into the classroom, where it would be much quieter, I reached for the door, but it was locked. I ended up waiting in the noisy hallway for fifteen minutes, which seemed like eternity. When the door was finally unlocked, I immediately bolted for a desk in the back. As the kids began to file in, I became more and more uncomfortable. The optimism I had experienced before had completely vanished and I was just trying to get through the class as discreetly as possible. Soon, however, the teacher started to call each student out and to have them introduce themselves. We had a meeting with this teacher recently and informed her that I have autism, which comes with extreme social anxiety. I was expecting her to skip me because I thought that she had actually understood my disability. Nevertheless, the time came when she asked me to stand up and introduce myself. I was mortified. I quickly shared my name, a hobby of mine, and an interesting fact about myself. I was proud of myself for having the courage to introduce myself on the spot like that, but I was also irate about what the teacher had just done to me.

My parents ended up calling her to clarify that she knew I had autism. She did indeed know but didn't quite understand why I needed special accommodations. She ended up asking my parents to write a "report", her words, about the symptoms of autism and why I needed her support. My parents, as well as I, were very insulted. We had already had a meeting with her in which she told us that she understood my needs and was eager to help. Apparently, however, she forgot all about that because she did the exact opposite of what she had agreed to.

Thus far, my transition into a mainstream high school was going horribly. Nonetheless, I made a commitment to myself that I would stick it out. I am not the type to quit, especially in the face of adversity. The second class I attended was history, which was ironically taught by the basketball coach. The first day went pretty well, for there were no unexpected incidences like the class before. As the classes progressed, however, things started to get out of hand. There was one day when I was on my way to history class, but when I got to the classroom, it was empty. Once again, the coach had forgotten to inform me about a change in the schedule. One of the biggest ways I stay on top of my autism is to always have a schedule, whether it is a school day or the weekend.

When I saw that the class was empty, I had no idea of what to do. I eventually headed over to my counselor's office, where he told me that the class was in the computer lab. There was no way I could attend that class because one of my biggest phobias is change, especially unexpected change. My heart was beating furiously. I told him that I was not fit to go to class and ended up reading for an hour and a half in the counselor's 10×10 foot office.

When I got home, I broke down and told my parents what had happened. I explained how painful and stressful the whole experience had been. They noticed that over the past week or two, I was becoming increasingly depressed. What a difference this was from earlier in the year, when I was very content with my life. We ultimately decided that public school was just not the way to go. We convened a meeting with Overlake, told them about all the things that had gone terribly awry, and decided to reinstate me there full-time. A huge weight was lifted off my shoulders.

I cannot explain to you the freedom that I felt the freedom from trying to live a normal life, the freedom from not having to be someone I'm not.

Although I was once again attending Overlake full time, I was still eligible to try out for my high school's basketball team.

After all the misfortunes that I had experienced with regards to playing basketball at that high school, I wasn't going to let that stop me from achieving my goal: making the varsity team. Unfortunately, one of the most devastating nights of my life occurred in November of 2006, the month basketball tryouts were to be held.

I anxiously counted the days until the tryouts were to be held, and finally the day had arrived. The tryouts were in two parts, which were to be held on back-to-back nights. I did my usual lengthy routine of getting prepared to play basketball, then I eagerly jumped into the car with my dad to drive to the school. I was ready. I was in the zone. I had been waiting my whole life for an opportunity like this and was ready to prove myself.

As I walked up to the gym inside the school, I was overwhelmed to see how many kids were there. At first I was hesitant to go in, but I was not going to let my anxiety take this chance away from me. As I walked in, I saw that the coaches were lining up all the kids. I walked up to the head coach and asked him what to do. He told me to just pick a line to stand in. When I was standing in line, I noticed that all the kids were holding a blue card. Right away, I knew something was amiss. The coach started calling out names for roll call. I waited and waited and waited, but he never called my name. As I look back on it, I can't help but think how ironic this was. The one time that I wanted to have my name called out in front of a crowd of people, it didn't happen.

After the roll call was over, the kids started to disperse into different groups. Once again, I walked up to the coach and asked him why my name hadn't been called. Without even looking me in the eye, he told me that I needed to be registered in able to try out and asked me for my registration card. I was dumbfounded. He had known me for more than five months and never once bothered to tell me that I needed to register in order to try out. I told him that I didn't have a card, and very bluntly he said, "You won't be able to try out tonight." I was furious. I was cheated by not having as much time to prove myself as all the other kids because, once again, the coach didn't care to communicate with me. He didn't care, period. He told me where to register and to come back tomorrow for the last night of the tryouts. As I walked out of the gym, my dad asked me what I was doing. I updated him about everything that had happened. He was in disbelief. He walked with me over to register for the next night, and then he drove me home. I felt like yelling at the top of my lungs, but as usual, I withdrew myself and resorted to crying.

The next night, as I was once again going through my usual routine to get ready to leave, I didn't really have any feelings toward trying out. I was still furious about the night before, and I was overwhelmingly numb towards walking back into the school gym, where so many bad memories had already occurred. I didn't have the drive or the mindset that I had the previous night, and I couldn't help but think to myself, that this was the day I had been waiting for for years. It was supposed to be a fun and enjoyable experience, not one shrouded in discrimination, hate and frustration.

My mom and dad both came with me to the school this time, and when I arrived I walked directly into the gym. I was put into a group with about nine other kids, and the coaches started putting us through some drills. Now, I had never played organized basketball before, and the coach knew this. Instead of taking this fact into account, he started calling out different plays that everyone knew but me. I had no idea of what to do and felt like an idiot wandering around the court like a lost dog. The coach got really angry with me and yelled at me to get off the court. Who did he replace me with? His son. He vehemently praised him left and right, telling everybody that they could learn something from watching his son play. I was disgusted. I had experienced a lot of prejudice throughout my life, but this was a new low.

ON THE OUTSIDE LOOKING IN

As the tryouts came to a close, although they lasted 2 hours, I ended up actively participating in drills, scrimmages, etc. for only about 10 minutes. When the tryouts were over, the coaches had all the players gather around them. They handed out envelopes to each kid, which told them if they had made it to one of the three teams (varsity, junior varsity, and the C team). With the envelope in my hand, I was hoping for the best but expecting the worse. Not surprisingly, I was cut. I did not make it to any of the teams.

Although I knew this moment was coming, I was in total shock. I couldn't grasp the fact that this was not a dream. It was, by far, the most devastating night of my life. I walked out of the gymnasium, went over to my parents, and broke down like never before. I thought that my life was over. I just could not fathom what had happened that night.

After my parents drove me home, I was repulsed just thinking about basketball. I took an hour long shower, kneeling down and sobbing. For the next five years, I had no interest in the game.

2007

In October of 2007, my family and I moved from Auburn, Washington, to Reno, Nevada. We all needed a change in weather while also breaking free from all the bad experiences that had occurred in Washington. I still had no friends, so it was an easy decision for my family and me to make. Moving to Reno was one of the best things that have ever happened to me. My depression improved significantly just from all the sunny weather. I felt like I had a brand-new life to start.

At this point, I was still not interested in playing organized basketball. Knowing that sports are a huge outlet for me, however, I turned my attention to football. I started working out furiously and studying the game for hours a day. I was going to make sure that football would not be reminiscent of my basketball tryouts.

Additionally, I had some newfound confidence due to being in a new community, and was hopeful that I would receive more support and accommodations from the school district than I did up in Washington. Now keep in mind, during this time I had no personal contact with anyone outside of my parents and sister, and the only time I left the house was to go to the gym. Well, I took a huge step forward one day in April of 2008 when my mom and I went to my local high school to meet with some of the staff, including the head football coach.

2008

As my first encounter with a high school coach was atrocious, I came into the meeting with no faith in the coach. During the meeting, he was informed that I had autism and that my goal was to play varsity football. He mentioned that he had coached a player with autism at his previous school. I didn't think much of this, for our first meeting with my basketball coach had also gone well. At any rate, during this meeting, I was enrolled in a weight lifting class that was led by the coach. He was told that I had not successfully attended a class in a public school for close to five years and that this was going to be a huge stepping stone for me. My mom and I left the meeting feeling optimistic, but that feeling didn't really mean much to me anymore.

ON THE OUTSIDE LOOKING IN

About a week later, the day had come to attend my weight lifting class. I was extremely anxious about it, but I knew that being in a physically active class would be much easier once I became involved in it. As my mom drove me to my class, I started to have a minor panic attack. I told myself that I had to persevere through this if I was committed to playing football. My mom walked into the class with me and stayed for about ten minutes while I calmed myself down and got used to my surroundings.

Now that I was in high school, having my mom in a class with me should have been somewhat embarrassing. The kids thought nothing of it though. It was a total 180 degrees of what had happened in Washington. The coach talked with my mom for a few minutes and told her how the class works and that he'd do his best to be as helpful as possible. Again, I thought nothing of this due to my past experiences. I'm happy to say, however, that I couldn't have been more wrong.

There were many times during my two years of playing varsity football where my coach would go above and beyond for me. Whenever I would have a panic attack or meltdown prior to going to practice, I would simply text my coach that I was having a rough time. Even though he was busy setting up for practice, he would still call me back and walk me through what my goals were, and that was to play football. He told me if I couldn't participate in practice then I couldn't participate in games. With blunt sincerity, he always knew how to motivate me, and how to aide in easing me out of my comfort zone.

There were even some instances where I would be having a meltdown in front of the school, feeling like I wasn't mentally strong enough to walk inside and make it to weight training. My coach would actually stop instructing the weight training class and come outside, sometimes accompanied by some of my teammates, to help me push through my struggles.

My face would be dripping with tears, and although somewhat embarrassing, it was oddly refreshing to let my peers know what I went through on an almost daily basis.

The next two years were some of the best in my life. Both years, I was able to play varsity football, working hard enough to earn a starting spot my second year, while also leading the team in sacks.

Although I literally never had a single conversation with any one of my teammates during my two years on the team, I became one of the most admired and respected players due to my tenacity and work ethic.

This football coach of mine, Jason Ehlen, is a prime example of what a role model should be, not just for kids with disabilities, but for all kids. His kindness, mixed with blunt observations of what I needed to do in order to accomplish my goals, made him one of the most respected men I have ever known.

When in doubt, reach out. You never know who may come along to help you fulfill your destiny.

As I look back on my experiences in school athletics, it is an unfortunate truth that the success of special needs students in this area relies heavily on the support they receive from their coaches. Even when students are fortunate enough to have such support, their goals can still be derailed if they don't have the secondary support of the teammates. Thankfully, however, if coaches truly support their players with disabilities, they will educate the teammates themselves, and keep them in check if ever they should start to antagonize or cause distress to these one-of-a-kind players.

I was very fortunate that during my time playing football, I had a coach who supported me and informed my teammates about my disability, and the repercussions for any ill-will towards me.

In December of 2008, a few days after Christmas, I lost my best friend, my guinea pig named Gilbert. When I woke up on Christmas morning, I ran over to his cage to give him his favorite breakfast, carrots. He would always come out of his wooden house that he would sleep under, squeaking uncontrollably for food. This particular morning, however, he didn't come out. I left the carrots in his cage, thinking that he was just sleeping in. A few hours later, I walked over to his cage to give him his Christmas present, fruit-flavored cookies. Again, he did not come out of his house. I thought that he was still sleeping in. The rest of the day went by without him coming out. The day after Christmas, he came out about three times, looking really exhausted. He ended up acting the same way the following day, so I finally took him out of his cage to see what the matter was. Except for looking exhausted, he seemed to be fine, so my mother and I asked our neighbor, who was a guinea pig expert, to come over and take a look. I had my mom show her Gilbert because I was too scared to hear what our neighbor might have to say. I distracted myself by watching a football game, but I couldn't help but think of the worst.

A couple minutes later, my mom came over to me and told me the news that I was so anxiously dreading. Gilbert had a tumor, and he seemed to only have a few hours left. I jumped up out of my chair and ran to my bedroom, trying to escape reality. I started to sob uncontrollably. My mom asked me if I wanted to see him, but I refused. I couldn't stand to see him that way. Finally, however, I agreed to hold him on my lap. For the next two hours, tears were pouring down my cheeks as Gilbert squirmed, twisted, and squeaked in pain. I tried my very best to comfort him, resting my hand on his back and lightly stroking him behind his ear when he seemed to need it. I remember wishing for him to let go as quickly as possible, for it absolutely broke my heart to pieces to see my best friend in so much pain and agony. Gilbert's fur was becoming increasing wet as my tears continued to flow. Finally, after what seemed like an eternity, he slowly started to drift away, as I gazed into his precious eyes that had brought me so much joy and happiness the past few years. Then, just like that, Gilbert's eyes slowly started to close. He was finally gone. To this day I find solace in the fact the I was the last thing he saw. This guinea pig saved my life, and I can only hope that he thought the same about me.

I ended up stayed with him for the rest of the day, about 8 hours. Lying next to him on my bedroom floor, I spent those 8 hours sobbing uncontrollably, stroking him on his head and never leaving his side. Feelings of despair, joy, thankfulness and grief continuously cycled through me as I reflected on all the beautiful memories that Gilbert Penny Lehmann gave to me. I will forever be grateful for what he did for me.

For the entire month of January, I was incapacitated due to the loss of Gilbert. I had just lost my best and only friend, and I did not know how I would survive. To this very day and as I write this, I still break down in tears whenever I think of him.

I had loved him with all my heart, and he had loved me back.

My Best Friend

I'm back after six months
That stone had gotten to me more than once
But now it's gone
Two days back was the whisper of "so long"

It was supposed to be temporary
But it's almost been two years
I dared not to go near it, just because of the fear
I was sick of wiping my face with my shirt to get the
tears
But as I write this, the tears start to appear

The pain hurts so much, and it will never go away
It's here to stay, but that's okay because it is the only
way
To remember the life that we had together, and to this
day
I beat myself with every single hit that I can take

I lashed out at you when all you wanted was to play
It was your way of telling me that you only had a few
days
Because after that all you did was try to get away

ON THE OUTSIDE LOOKING IN

You hid from me, but I brushed it off; a mistake that
turned so grave

I was so stupid to take for granted the life you gave
to me
And when I finally asked you what was wrong, it was
just too late
This wasn't fate, it was God's way to turn my life into
misery
I love you so much I cannot even begin to say
All of the things that I would do to spend time with
you today
You were my best friend, but like I said God took that
away

I try not to think of you; No, I love you too much
When I do my heart gets crushed, the pain, it's just
too much
I guess it's self centered, it's my emotional crutch
But this is what I signed up for, the second that we
touched

I'll never forget you Gilbert, you turned me into a man
I was and always will be your biggest fan
People don't understand how you could be my best
friend
My only friend, and in the end I wished it was pretend

RUSSELL LEHMANN

I'll never forget you Gilbert, you are in my heart until
the end
And the end will just begin, when I see you once again

Gilbert Penny Lehmann

*"There is no greater sorrow than to recall happiness
in times of misery."*

~ Danté Alighieri

2009

In July of 2009, my football team was scheduled to attend a high school football camp for three days. The camp was in Gold Beach, Oregon, over 450 miles away. I was really excited about the camp, but as the date came closer and closer, I started to feel less excited and much more anxious. I had never spent one night away from home, except for being in the hospital. My coach had called me the best defensive end in northern Nevada earlier that summer, and I knew I couldn't let my teammates down. When the time had come to leave, I hesitantly gave my mom a big hug, and slowly walked onto the school bus. The ride was excruciating. There were two kids to a seat, and it took over twelve hours to get to the camp.

When we finally arrived, we set up our inflatable mattresses and belongings inside the local high school where we were staying. There were at least eight other schools that were there. This was very overwhelming for me, for each player only had about five square feet of personal space. The very first night was very difficult for me. I had become very anxious, and I didn't know anyone enough to help make me feel comfortable. I was finally able to calm myself down and go to sleep. The next morning, however, I had a panic attack. I kept it all bottled inside because I didn't want anyone to know that I was scared of being away from home. I called my mom and gave her an update about what was going on. I told her that I really wanted to come home and that I didn't think that I could handle three more days of this. She told me to use my coping skills and to just relax for the moment. About five minutes after we ended our call, my coach waved me over from across the room. I hesitantly stood up from my bed and walked over to him. He told me that my mom had called to let him know what my condition was. We took a walk out of the school and over to his RV, where we sat down and talked for a good forty-five minutes. There was a beautiful view of the ocean in front of us, and the smell of the saltwater really helped calm me down. We talked about all the great things that I had accomplished since joining the football team and how I had found the courage to accomplish this feat. He gave me the option of going home early if I didn't think I could handle it. Even though I really wanted to go home, I was very opposed to the idea. I did not want to let anyone down, especially my coach and the team itself. For the next three days, I was able to block all the negative thoughts and worries in my head and ended up having some of the best days of my life. The only thing that I could not stop dreading was the torturous twelve-hour bus ride home!

I have recently come to realize that there has not been one risk that I've taken in my life that has not ended up benefiting me tremendously, and with this knowledge I move forward in life with confidence and my head held up high.

At the end of the 2009 football season, I had made tremendous progress with my social anxiety and communication skills. Over those two years of playing football, which were some of the best in my life, I had really enjoyed the camaraderie of my teammates, even though I barely spoke, and mostly just listened to my teammates' conversations and laughed at their jokes.

I was't able to play at the level everyone expected me to that year because I had lost all the cartilage in my big right toe. Every time that I took a step, bone was rubbing on bone, and it was excruciatingly painful. However, there was no way I was going to sit out the season, so I gritted my teeth and was able to play in every game.

I finished leading the team in sacks, while also leading all defensive ends in tackles. I had surgery two months after the season ended.

RUSSELL LEHMANN

At the end of the season banquet in November, our coach brought each player up, one by one, and gave a short thirty-second speech about them. I was waiting and waiting for my name to be called, but it turned out that I was the last one chosen. I walked over to the coach, and he gave an unbelievable six-minute speech about all the obstacles that I had overcome and how proud he was of me. This was definitely one of the proudest moments of my life. Near the end of the speech, my coach started to tear up, describing me as a role model for all the kids out there with autism. A couple tears started to fall from my own eyes. It meant so much to me that he gave that speech. Nobody had ever done something like that before. To top it off, a few moments later, I was named to the Nevada All-State Academic Team. I will definitely never forget that night.

2010

In June of 2010 I decided to play college football. I was working out with one of the top athletic training agencies on the west coast and was very excited about my future and the potential it held. During this time, my trainer told me that I needed to put on a lot more weight. I was 180lbs, and he wanted me to get up to at least 200lbs. This meant that I needed to start drastically eating more food while also training hard six days a week. I was happy to hear this because I love to eat, but was also hesitant about the idea because I liked the shape I was in and didn't want to gain any excess fat. My trainer reassured me that gaining fat was unlikely, and even if I did, a little fat would actually be good. I started to hesitantly eat more food, probably around 5,500 calories a day, and in the next 10 months my weight shot up to

202lbs. I was as strong and as fast as ever, however I could tell that I did gain a tiny amount of fat around my waist. I still had a six-pack, but I was obsessed with my body looking absolutely perfect that the minute amount of fat I did gain was becoming intolerable for me to live with. However, I continued with my regimen because I knew that if I wanted to play college football I would have to make some sacrifices (irrational as they were) when it came to how my body looked.

I took highschool classes online and played for two years as a starter on the varsity football team despite debilitating socail anxiety.

2011

When 2011 came around, I was really excited about playing college football. I would have to move out of my parents' house in June and live by myself two hundred miles away. I thought that I was ready to take on this challenge, but when June came closer and closer, my family and I began to realize how unrealistic the situation was. We had a lengthy discussion about the move, and I had come to terms that there was no way I was going to be able to live by myself two hundred miles away without knowing anyone around, all while having to attend school, which I was deathly afraid of. Even though it broke my heart and crushed my dream, I ended up deciding not to play college football. However, I was somewhat comforted by the fact that I wouldn't have been able to play anyway, because my big toe that I had surgery on was becoming increasingly painful again. If I were to play, I would risk severely injuring it, with the risk of having to have the joints fused together.

Later that year, in March of 2011, I was set to go on my the very first date of my life, at the age of 20. I was extremely excited because I didn't have anyone to talk to or hang out with besides my family. I had psyched myself up the whole week before the date and was ready to give it my best shot. It was one of the happiest weeks of my life. The morning of the date, however, I received a text from her saying that she had been hit with an ear infection and would not be able to make it. I replied by saying that I hope she recovers soon and to let me know when she wants to reschedule. After a few days, I had not heard from her, so I sent her another text, asking how she felt. I never heard from her again. I was crushed. I thought that I was finally encountering some normalcy in my life, but just like that, it was ripped away from me. I went into a deep depression for about a week, spending the days crying under the covers of my bed. I felt as if I had known this woman (who I had never met in person before) my whole life, probably a result of reactive attachment as I had not come into contact with a female for over 10 years.

I'm a Fool for You

I've already fallen for you, but I don't even know you
We haven't even met, but somehow I adore you
I can't get you out of my head; thoughts of you are
stuck like glue
The pain is starting to progress; I am depressed
without you

We're supposed to meet each other, but something's
telling me we won't
I've got to get this mess together; I'm going insane
being alone
I'm waiting in the rain for you; I guess that I'll go
home
The flowers drop to the ground, as I trace back this
lonely road

I need to be with you, I'll wait for you, just to be
cruel
A broken heart will be my death; I'll put away the
rope and stool
I'll throw my whole life away, if it means that we'll be
two
I'm a fool, but I don't care, this is all that I can do

ON THE OUTSIDE LOOKING IN

Later that year, in June, I ended up going on my very first date with a girl named Danielle. I was very nervous. Once we saw each other, however, it was amazing how much I opened up and talked. I had never talked that much to a stranger in my whole life. The date ended up going great, and we met again a few days later to have lunch in the park. I talked even more this time. It was amazing how comfortable I felt around her. It was another great date, and we decided to hang out again later that week. Two days later, I called her and asked what she wanted to do. She hesitantly told me that she didn't think we should see each other again. When I asked her why, she responded by telling me that I reminded her too much of her ex-boyfriend and that she had met someone else.

Once again, my heart was ripped out and stepped on. She was the only person I could even come close to calling my friend, and I did not want to lose her. We stopped communicating with each other once she told me her decision was final. I was baffled. Back then it seemed like whenever something was going right for me, it turned out to be just a joke. I ended up going into another deep depression, staying in my room for hours a day, thinking about her and crying nonstop. I hated my life. I always had faith that my life would someday get easier. Whenever that seemed to happen, however, it took a turn for the worse.

On July 1, 2011, I moved out of my parents' house and into my own apartment. This was an enormous step for me. Although I was unsure if I could succeed in this endeavor of mine, I was at the same time excited to become much more independent and to have a place I could call my own.

During my very first night in my apartment, after my family was done helping me move in, I received a text from Danielle. It had been over two weeks since we stopped talking, and I had finally started to get over her. She asked me how I liked my apartment and told me she was happy for me. After texting for a while, I ended up asking her if she wanted to come over and check it out sometime. She excitedly said yes, and she came over two days later. The night she came over, we ended up talking for four hours. That was, by far, the longest I had ever talked to anyone my whole life. She told me that things weren't working out with the other guy, and so we made plans to see each other again in a couple of days. After about three more dates, I asked her if she wanted to be together (being that this was the first dating experience of my life, I was, as you would expect, extremely naive). With a big smile, she said yes and told me how special I was to her. This was one of the happiest moments in my life. It was so surreal I could not believe it. We started to hang out more often, every date being better than the last. Before I moved, I was worried about being depressed and lonely in my apartment. Having a girlfriend, though, was all I needed to live a happy life.

The next month seemed like one of the best in my life. Things had indeed worked out for me, and I thanked God every night for that. One day, I texted Danielle and asked her if she wanted to go out to dinner one night. She told me that she couldn't because she already had plans. She also told me, quite bluntly, that she had decided to go back to her abusive ex-boyfriend. She didn't think we should see each other again. My heart stopped. I was in complete shock. She had told me repeatedly that she was never getting back together with her ex, and due to my naivety and lack of social interaction, I put complete trust in her words.

This blow did me in. I felt like my life was over, and for the first time in my life I began experiencing suicidal ideations. Even though I would never pull the trigger on myself, I was craving for a gun. I was, however, thinking of seriously hurting her ex. He was extremely abusive to her and controlled every aspect of her life. I was at such a low point, that I thought that if I ended up getting arrested for doing something extreme, I would have been glad to embrace jail or even prison. At least then I would have structure in my day and be around other people, instead of sitting alone all day in my apartment. I was so devastated that I cannot begin to describe my feelings. I did, however, try to in a letter I wrote to Danielle.

Dear Danielle,

I do not want this letter to cause you any guilt, but I need you to know the pain I am feeling. I am not lying when I say you are one of the best things that have ever happened to me. Yes, we have only known each other for 6 weeks, but I know a special person when I see one. I don't know if I have told you this, but 8 years ago I was admitted to a hospital in Seattle to help treat my OCD, depression and anxiety. I was in there for 5 weeks of pure hell. I would have much preferred being in jail for those weeks. At least then I wouldn't have any mental disabilities destroying my life.

The last time I had a friend was in 2001. The past 10 years have been excruciatingly lonely and depressing, along with feelings that would take years of explaining for someone to understand. Hundreds of times I have cried myself to sleep at night, hoping and praying that I would soon find a friend.

When we met for the first time on June 11, it was my first experience hanging out with someone besides my family in over a decade. I was extraordinarily nervous before I actually saw you. But when I did see you, there was something about you that made me open up and talk like no one else has made me before. I know that you thought that I was really shy that night, but I totally exceeded my expectations of how much I thought I'd talk that night. I was on cloud 9 that night, as well as every other time we have hung out. We had only met once, but it was such a huge step for me in my life that I was starting to think would never come.

When you texted me a couple of days after our second date, explaining that you had found someone else that you connected with more, I was in so much pain that it was indescribable. I know that you did nothing wrong and that you had every right to choose to stop seeing me. After 2 ½ weeks, I was just starting to get over you. Yes I added you on Facebook, but the very first night at my new place you texted me for the first time in 2 weeks. It led to me asking if you ever wanted to come over and check my place out. You said yes, and that night we ended up talking for 4 hours, the longest I had ever talked to someone. About a week later I asked if you wanted to be together and you said yes. That was one of the happiest moments of my life. You had told me multiple times how bad your ex treats you and that you were not going to get back together with him. If I had known that you still had feelings for him, I would have never asked you to be committed with me.

You also told me that he was being very nice all of a sudden just because he was jealous of you seeing someone else. I expressed to you my fear of losing you, and was reassured when you told me that we would eventually end up being together and that everything would work out. About 12 days ago, you told me that you were not ready to be in a relationship and that you needed to take some time to just clear your head of everything. You told me how your ex kept contacting you saying that he wanted to get back together, and flipped out every time you would mention us. I was more than willing to give you the space and time that you needed to get things straight. On July 22, we went to the marina to just hang out and chat. You brought up the topic of our relationship and asked me how I felt about it. You even asked me if I was worried that you and your ex would get back together. I told you that I knew you two would not get back together, but that my fear of that was always in the back of my mind. I hope that at this time you had not already made up your mind about your ex and you, because if you had, I really wish you would have told me then and there. I was still very excited about meeting your family, and was really looking forward to taking you out to dinner.

On Monday I asked if you wanted to hang out on Tuesday. All of a sudden, however, and out of the blue, you told me that you were seeing your ex again. You told me that deep down, you really want it to work with him, even though you're sure it won't. I was devastated and I still am. You broke my heart Danielle.

I don't want you to think that I am writing this letter out of spite and that I want you to feel guilty. I just really want to tell you the absolute truth about how I feel.

ON THE OUTSIDE LOOKING IN

You have been the reason I have done so well living by myself. You often ask if I get lonely. I do, but texting with you every day and looking forward to hanging out with you was all that I needed. Like I said before, you are the only true friend I have and have had. I cannot express the feelings I have about you entering my life.

I am not trying to win the sympathy vote in hopes that you will come back. I want you to follow your heart. I just want to let you know that I will wait in case things don't work out, but obviously it is your choice if you ever want to see me again or hang out. I'll always have my phone with me in case you ever want to talk.

Sincerely,

Russell

I spent a very long time composing that letter while trying to capture all my feelings in it. My keyboard was soaked with tears once I had finished. I was not myself after this whole ordeal. I mentally broke down multiple times a day. No one could understand the pain I was feeling. I lost my only friend I'd had in over ten years and knew I would never see her again. She might have just as well died.

I ended up entering a deep depression, which lasted for months. I couldn't bear living in my apartment by myself, so in August, a little over a month after I moved out of my parents' house, I moved back in. I would stay at my place for a couple of hours during the day every so often, but that was it.

Untitled

Monday was the day that you paralyzed me with pain
Destroying my whole world with the most unbearable
strain
Of depression that I maintained for weeks without any
gains
All the while leaving a stain on my heart that you
ripped and maimed
That day was the closest that I had ever maintained
The thought of having my brains rain
Upon my lifeless body from a colt .45 aimed
At the origin of all things gained, at the origin of all
my pain

You tore me up, but now I'm coming back stronger
Yes, I'm still depressed, but yet I am no longer
Unsure of my will to live on, an idea so heavily pon-
dered
Those thoughts are collected and are now much calmer

ON THE OUTSIDE LOOKING IN

I sang a song so somber
But the harp's strings are being pulled no longer
What you did was neither right nor wrong
You killed the feelings I had forever longed for

They say that everything happens for a reason
Hinting that everything will soon work ITSELF OUT
But what if that everything goes back on its promise?
Like my everything did, burying my heart six feet down

I dream of seeing you again, but I know that dream will
not come true
I'm moving on without you, for I now know I'm too
good for you
You made me want to kill from all the sadness that you
brewed
But the only thing I will kill are the memories of being
with you

Later that August I had to give up my dream of
playing college football once and for all due to my toe.
It had become so painful that I was scheduled to have
a second surgery on it in September. Although I was
deeply disheartened to have to give up my dream, I

was somewhat relieved that I could go back to eating normally and hopefully lose some of the excess fat that I had gained in the past year due to my training. However, I soon became so obsessed about losing the excess fat that I started to rigorously decide what I could and could not eat. This situation evolved extremely rapidly, and soon after I was diagnosed with anorexia and body dysmorphic disorder (BDD).

I had always been obsessed about my body image, however when I stopped training for college football, this obsession became increasingly worse, and later, in 2012, it would become detrimental to my quality of life.

On September 23, 2011, I had surgery on my right big toe for the second time. A few months prior, I started receiving the same excruciating amount of pain that I did in 2009. My doctor gave me a Kevlar insert to wear in my shoe so that my toe would not bend when walking or running. This immediately relieved me of any pain that I had. However, once again things just didn't seem to go my way. It turned out that before I had received my implant, I had subconsciously altered the way I walked, due to the pain I was feeling. This eventually ended up in me fracturing my left foot. I wore a walking boot for six weeks and even used a state-of-the-art ultrasound bone healing system. When the time came to take the boot off, I was extremely excited. However, when the doctor took an x-ray of my foot to make sure that the bone had healed, it turned out that it did not heal at all. I cannot describe how frustrated I was. Adding to that, I was set to have my second surgery on my toe in the near future. This time around, the cause of the pain in my toe was due to large amounts of bone spurs growing underneath the previous incision mark. In the weeks leading up to my surgery, I chose not to wear the boot on my fractured left foot, but instead decided to wait until after the surgery to wear it, attempting to kill two birds with one stone. In early October, I wore a boot on each foot and prayed that everything would heal successfully this time.

Over the next couple of weeks, the fracture in my left foot had finally healed enough for me to take the boot off. However, the progress with my toe was far inferior. The doctor who had performed my surgery was the best in Northern Nevada, and I was very confident that my toe would never bother me again. During my post-op check up, he told me that I would be able to resume my normal activities (i.e. basketball, sprinting, weight lifting, etc) in about three to four months, yet this did not happen until seven months after the operation, and with tremendous pain, too.

My toe never did heal properly. To this day I have about 30% less flexibility in it than my other toe, and it

RUSSELL LEHMANN

turns inward when I bend it instead of bending straight. I have to tape it 24/7, for it causes me pain every single day, sometimes to the point where I can't even put any pressure on it. I recently had a doctor tell me that I had "the ugliest toe [he'd] ever seen". However, I continue to work out hard, play basketball, and sprint almost every day because of how well it helps calm my anxiety and OCD. The doctor had warned me that pushing my toe like I do every day could end up with the joint fusing itself together at some point, but I try to live in the moment and do what is best for me now.

2012

In early 2012, my eating disorder started to destroy my life. I severely restricted what I ate and started to deny myself food whenever I was hungry. I started to work out for more than two hours a day, and even then I was still afraid of eating. I started to count calories with vigor and cut out about 50% of the foods that I used to eat, even if they were healthy. All I cared about was consuming as little amount of calories as possible, while also strictly limiting any saturated fats that I ate. I aimed to eat less than 2 grams of saturated fat before dinner. To put that into perspective, a man who burns approximately 3,800–4,500 calories a day, as I do, consumes an average of 40 grams of saturated fat per day.

Soon I was becoming unable to go to the gym everyday due to lack of energy. I was extremely weak when it came to lifting weights, and this realization of how weak I was becoming led me into a severe depression. Every day I would wake up with my sights set on working out that morning, even though I wasn't nearly refreshed as I should have been after sleeping an uninterrupted nine hours. Half the time I failed to go to the gym. I just felt like laying on the couch all day, plus I was becoming afraid to leave the house again, which was a very worrisome sign for me. There were many times when I would get ready to go work out and actually drive into the parking lot of the gym, just to break down in tears and head back home.

This depression lasted for over two months, and these episodes kept repeating themselves over and over. I began to lose weight drastically, falling all the way down to 150lbs (I am 6'2" tall). At this particular point in time, I was actually happy that I was losing so much weight, because I knew that I wasn't gaining any fat.

When I was playing high school football in 2008 and 2009, every week we would have a team dinner on the night before our game. I didn't have an eating disorder back then, and I would eat so much on these nights that I can't possibly fathom ever eating that much again in my life. When we went out for pizza, I would have anywhere from six to nine slices, along with pasta and other side dishes. Sometimes I would eat half an apple pie, too. I ate around 4,000 calories on the nights we had our team dinners, and I wasn't worried at all about gaining any fat.

In addition, every morning I would have four pieces of peanut butter toast, with an extreme amount of peanut butter. This equaled out to about 1,100 calories just for breakfast. I was still in extremely good shape and I never gained one ounce of fat.

Once my eating disorder began to get out of hand though, I cut peanut butter entirely out of my diet, even though it is one of my favorite foods. I switched my breakfast from four pieces of peanut butter toast to one bowl of the lowest calorie cereal. For lunch, I would again just have one bowl of cereal. In previous years, I would either have a large peanut butter and jelly sandwich, or something else of that caliber.

Even though I had 5 percent body fat during this time (the average male body fat is 15-22 percent), I was still very hesitant to take off my shirt when going to the beach or swimming in a pool. I work out so much that when I do take a day off, my metabolism is extremely high and I'm usually very hungry. However, as my eating disorder began to grow stronger and stronger, I began to starve myself on the days I did not work out. I was losing a lot of weight (6 lbs. in ten days), and my family was worried about me. They could definitely tell that I was losing a lot of my muscle mass. I was so afraid of gaining the littlest amount of fat that the feeling of being hungry was much better than feeling the mental anguish of my OCD after I would eat. Deep down, I knew that I could eat anything

I want and still have the same physique, but the pain of obsession was just too much to handle. I started to hallucinate with regards to my body image, feeling fat building and drooping down instantaneously on my chest after I would eat. I rationally knew that there was no way possible for that to happen, but my OCD overrode any sanity that I had left during those days.

I absolutely loved pizza, but it hurt my brain too much to even have one slice. My favorite dinner was spaghetti and sausage, but I decided to just have plain spaghetti noodles while my family ate the regular meal. I wouldn't eat cheese of any kind, ground beef, turkey and yogurt (unless they are fat-free), nuts, protein bars, the list goes on and on. Every single food that I had cut out of my diet was one of my favorite foods to eat. I used to eat them with no problem, and I began to greatly miss those care-free days.

In June of 2012, exactly one year after going on my first date with Danielle, I went on a date with a girl named AJ, who I also met online. We met each other at the bank of the Truckee River in downtown Reno and walked and talked for a good hour and a half. She already knew that I had autism, and was very non-discriminatory towards the fact, which I was pleasantly surprised by. It was a beautiful evening, and as we walked along the side of the river we talked about all sorts of things. Poetry, autism, family, relationships, hobbies, almost everything under the moon. Her personality was a total 180 from mine, which I really enjoyed, for it brought out the outgoing side of me. She was very hyper and always had a smile on her face. She told jokes almost constantly, but also knew how to listen when the time came for it. She was also very sarcastic, which I loved, even though I sometimes didn't know when to believe her. After we talked we decided to go to a movie, ending up hanging out for about four hours. At the end of the date we both happily agreed to see each other again.

We ended up seeing each other the next three nights, which were incredibly enjoyable. We walked all over downtown Reno, wandered through the casinos, went out to dinner, and watched the sun set at the Boca Reservoir in California. And that was just on one night.

In the past when I would date, I tended to attach myself to the person very quickly because I didn't have any friends or any other peers to interact with. Basically, I used to be a desperate man, however I'm not ashamed to say that. We as humans are naturally social creatures, so it should come as no surprise that I was indeed very eager to have personal interactions due to being isolated from society for so long. Even if half the time I didn't want to interact with others, I still needed to in order to properly grow and develop as a man.

I quite rapidly took a strong liking to AJ. She was extremely mature for her age yet also knew how to have a lot of fun. I couldn't find a single fault with her, or so I thought. Today, looking back, I realized I was taking a liking to the socialization, not the woman.

On our second date, we were watching the Women's National Bowling Championship at the National Bowling Stadium in downtown Reno. We were talking about relationships, and towards the end of the conversation I asked her how she felt about me. After laughing uncomfortably for a moment and being very hesitant in trying to answer, she quickly leaned over and kissed me. "That's how I feel" she said.

Even though we had only known each other for a little more than a day, I was addicted. Aside from my brief experience with Danielle, this was my first taste of true, natural socialization in over a decade. I woke up the next morning with the most incredible feeling.

AJ was very spontaneous, which is the exact opposite of what I am. Being on the spectrum, I find comfort in having every single part of my day scheduled days in advance, and I do not get tired of having the same exact routine every day. However, being exposed to this kind of spontaneity opened my eyes to a whole new world. A world that I knew I didn't fit in, but which was amazing to get a taste of. The day after our fourth date AJ texted me and, out of the blue, asked me if I wanted to go to San Francisco with her in a few days. I was stunned by this invitation, but was enthralled nonetheless. We had not even known each other a week, yet I immediately texted her back saying that I would love to go. Understand that before I met AJ, my life consisted of nothing but working out and sitting at home. When I would hang out with her, however, it was so uplifting and I experienced the type of fun that I had never had before, and which I craved vehemently for years. Being with her was, as I alluded to before, akin to being on a drug. I felt so naturally high around her and wanted to be with her every second of every day, for it certainly beat just sitting at home doing nothing. I would later find out, however, that the drug I was on was toxic.

When it came time to tell my parents about our decision to go to San Francisco, I did not ask for their permission or approval, as I was an adult capable of making my own choices. I just flat out told them my feelings about AJ and that we decided to take a one night trip to San Francisco to just relax and have a change of scenery. They had their concerns, and rightly so, for our relationship was evolving far too rapidly. However, being the accepting and supporting parents that they are, the did not bar me from going. With this, I started to pack for the trip with feelings of such indescribable excitement.

A few mornings later I picked up AJ at 6:00 am and we set off on our journey. I had only been away from home once in my whole life, and that was when my high school football team went to Gold Beach, Oregon for a football training camp back in 2009. I can't put into words how keyed up I was. We had a safe drive all the way to our hotel, which we surprisingly found with ease. However, since we couldn't check in until 2:00pm we decided to make an impromptu visit to the San Francisco Zoo first, another one of AJ's spontaneous ideas that pushed me outside of my comfort zone. We ultimately had a great time there, and I felt like we really connected and bonded in a way that hadn't happened yet.

After the zoo we went back to the hotel and ordered dinner. We had Chinese food, something that I never eat if I don't work out that day. Much to my surprise, however, I ate it without worry or guilt and enjoyed it very much. There was something about being with AJ that made all of my problems go away. After dinner we headed back out to Fisherman's Wharf. It was unbelievably busy and very loud, however this did not bother me one bit. This was the magic that I had so much enjoyed when I was with AJ. I was a totally different person. I guess you could say I was what some people consider "normal". I was not the least bit overwhelmed, and my energy level was very high, telling jokes and talking with AJ almost non-stop throughout the night. We also went to Ghirardelli Square and Pier 39 that night.

When we arrived at Fisherman's Wharf earlier in the evening, there was absolutely nowhere to park. After about 20 minutes of driving in circles around the various blocks, we finally found a spot. However, when exited the car we realized that the spot was just a little too small, for about six inches of my trunk was hanging over the red curb area. We took a chance and left it there, thinking that there was no way they would tow the car, especially since my tires weren't even touching the red. This ultimately proved disastrous, however.

Around 10pm we headed back to the car. We forgot to look at the cross street that we parked on, so finding the car would soon become increasingly difficult. It also didn't help that every street in San Francisco looked exactly alike to us. After wandering around searching for the car for over an hour, we finally came to the conclusion that it must have been towed.

I ended up calling my mom and telling her the situation. She did some detective work and found out that indeed the car had been towed. AJ and I then decided to take a taxi back to our hotel, and the next morning I had to head down to the impound lot and pick up my car.

I woke up early the next morning so that I could relax a little before having to venture out on my own to pick up the car. I had never done anything like this alone before, especially in a busy city that I had never been to before. Although the idea seemed very tempting and comforting, I ultimately did not want to ask AJ to come with me because she was exhausted, and I knew that I was an adult capable of accomplishing this task. Deep down I also saw this daunting task of venturing into downtown San Francisco alone as a test, a test that I had to at least attempt to take on my own, especially if I was ever going to live the independent life that I dreamed of.

I soon left the hotel, and after spending about 15 minutes trying to hail down a cab, I was on my way to pick up the car. Much to my surprise, I was very talkative with the cab driver, asking him if he liked driving the crazy streets of San Francisco as his job, if he liked living there, etc. I felt like a totally different person while out and about on my own. Looking back on this memory, I can say that this was my first glimpse into the immense potential of sociability that I would soon discover resided within me.

Once I was dropped off at the impound, I thanked the taxi driver for the ride and walked inside. After about thirty minutes I was ushered out to the car lot in the back, and there I saw a sight that instantly relieved all the built-up stress within me, my car. I joyfully hopped in and eventually found my way back to the hotel. Suffice to say that I passed this test of independence, something I was extremely pleased with myself about.

We packed up when I got back to the room and soon left the hotel in order to explore more of the city before heading back home. Aj had spotted a restaurant that served crepes the day before and really wanted to go there for breakfast. This was a big change for me because every morning during this time period I would eat the same thing, one bowl of Multi-Grain Cheerios. However, I knew that if I wanted to be in a relationship with someone, I would frequently have to step out of my comfort zone. I happily agreed to take her there, and I ate my crepe without the least bit of anxiety. It was such an amazing feeling. I felt like I was destroying every obstacle that had ever been in my way. The same thing happened at lunch, for at home I used to always have another bowl of cereal. We decided to go to Boudin Bakery and I ordered a vegetarian delight sandwich, while AJ let me have some of her Caesar salad. This day also consisted of me having a piece of chocolate, something that up until then I hadn't eaten in years. I felt like I was living a normal life, and I absolutely loved it.

Before we left to go home, we managed to go to the Aquarium of the Bay, which was a blast. We also had time to explore the city more and to do some shopping. When four o'clock came around, we decided to head home. There was a lot of traffic when we were leaving the city and passing over the Oakland Bay Bridge, so we started to sing and dance (as well as we could in a car) to the radio. This was unlike anything I had ever done before with someone outside of my family. I had broken out of my secluded shell and was living the life that I had always dreamed of, and it felt absolutely amazing. I ended up dropping AJ off at her house at around 8:30pm, and arrived at my house at 9 o'clock.

Once I got home I was exhausted and went straight to bed. I didn't wake up until 1:00 in the afternoon and was still very worn out. AJ texted me later in the day and asked if I could meet her at the local marina that night. I had thought we would both want to take a day or two break from seeing each other to just relax, but I agreed to meet up with her anyway.

When I arrived at the marina, I saw AJ sitting quietly on the beach. I could immediately tell something was wrong. I walked over to where she was and sat down next to her. When I asked her what was wrong, she just shrugged her shoulders without uttering a word. I knew that she had been having issues at work and with her family, but I really didn't know to what extent. I told her that I was there for her if she ever wanted to talk, and as I said this tears starting rolling down her cheeks. Out of the blue, she told me that she wanted to go bowling, so we left and went straight to the bowling alley.

We had a great time there, and I was able to make her smile and laugh a couple of times. It felt really good to see a smile on her face again, for I had never seen her that quiet prior to going bowling. We played two games and then we left. As I walked her to her car, she opened up a little and told me that she just needed a break from everything. To my dismay, we agreed not to text each other for a couple of days so that she could try to clear her head. With this we both got into our cars and left to go home.

Three days later I sent her a text asking her how she was and if she felt any better. She responded "Same". This one-word answer turned into a pattern on her part the whole week. I would try to bring up subjects that required lengthier answers, but at the most she would send back three or four words, which was very unlike her. I asked her on Wednesday of that week if she wanted to go on a picnic that Saturday night. My aunt, uncle, and grandmother were coming into town that night and I knew that I would be overwhelmed, so I really wanted to just escape and go out. She answered back "Maybe" and I just responded by telling her to let me know when she makes a decision. I was sure she was going to say yes, so I spent a lot of time searching for the perfect park by the Truckee River and planning out the whole night. I was really looking forward to that night, and a big part of that was because we hadn't seen each other in eight days.

I personally need a lot of structure in my life, and knowing what I am going to do each and every day is a big comfort for me. I know now that in a relationship you have to give and take, but I was becoming increasingly anxious because I didn't know if I would get the chance to escape the commotion of my relatives coming into town, and I certainly didn't want to go out by myself. When Thursday night had rolled around, I had still not heard from her. I decided to wait until she got off work that night and called her to ask again if she would like to hang out that Saturday. She didn't pick up, which was very unusual for her, so I ended up leaving a message. I never received a call back. I sent her a text afterwards to let her know that I had called, but in the next 24 hours she didn't text back. AJ usually responded to texts within a couple of minutes, and the fact that she wasn't returning my calls or texts made me extremely disappointed and frightened because I felt like I was losing her, while also losing the freedom from my struggles that I felt came with her. I tried texting her again on Friday night and once again did not receive an answer. I was starting to go crazy. I couldn't help but think that she didn't want to see me again. I started to constantly look back at every little thing I did that could have possibly made her mad or annoyed with me, but I couldn't find one. At this point I started to become very depressed and angry.

I liked AJ so much and couldn't stand the thought of not seeing her again. So on Saturday afternoon I texted her once again and asked her if everything was okay. No response. Two hours later I sent her a final text asking about going out that night, for I really had my heart set on it. Once again, no response. This literally crushed my heart. I wasn't just depressed at this point, I was devastated. My mind was telling me that our relationship was over, but in no way did I want to believe that.

On Sunday afternoon I called her with a different phone, thinking that she would pick up if she didn't think that it was me calling. This worked, and I finally got my chance to talk to her. I first asked her how she was, and she told me that she was great. I went on to ask her if she received any of my texts or calls and she told me that she hadn't. I was dumbfounded and relieved at the same time. I told her that I had wanted to go out with her the previous night, to which she confirmed to me that she hadn't received any of my attempted communications. She went on to say that she was shopping with her mom and that she would call me back in a few hours. I told her I was fine with that and we said goodbye and ended the conversation. I felt such relief knowing that she wasn't blowing me off, but instead just didn't receive my texts or calls. In the back of my mind I was certainly suspicious, but I knew that she wasn't lying about being out shopping because I could hear multiple voices in the background. She also sounded very genuinely surprised when I told her about the texts I had sent. I waited the rest of the night to hear back from her, never letting my phone be more than three feet away from me. As the night went on, I still hadn't heard back from her and by 10:00 I was once again starting to become very depressed. I now knew that she was indeed blowing me off and I couldn't stand the thought of losing her.

I became increasingly depressed with every moment that passed and was now lying on my bed sobbing uncontrollably. I truly believed that she was the best thing that had happened to me, and up until that point in my life, she probably was. She showed me all life had to offer, and she rescued me from my seclusion. My mind started to race like never before and my depression was now worse than at any point in my life before. This Sunday night was one of the worst in my life. I felt like I wanted to end it all. The mental pain I was experiencing was so immense that all I could think about was sticking a gun in my mouth and pulling the trigger or slicing my throat. I even started to cut the top of my hands with a small pocketknife, something that in a million years I never thought I'd do. That night was the first time in my life that I was genuinely suicidal, and I wasn't ashamed of it. I had been through so much in my life already that I felt like I didn't have any more strength in me to persevere anymore. During that time in my life I felt like my life had been nothing but one hurdle after another in which there was no finish line. I had a bitter and pessimistic outlook, for so many bad things had happened to me and so few good things. At least, that's what it seemed like during this time of severe distress. I started to cuss at God, wondering why I couldn't just be a "normal" person and why he was putting me through all of this chaos without ever receiving the least bit of a reward. Looking back, I realize how wrong I was.

At this point during the night my mom and dad had come into my room and told me that they were extremely worried about me. They wanted me to make a commitment to them that I wouldn't hurt myself in any way. For the first time in my life I told them that I couldn't make that commitment. I told them that I wanted to kill myself and I truly did want to die at that moment in time. I had given up, the pain was just too much to handle. I could tell that my parents were horrified by my answer, and they strictly told me that if I did not commit to not hurting myself that I would have to be taken to the ER. They also gave me the option of either sleeping in their room that night or having my dad sleep in my room.

My head started to spin like crazy and I couldn't think at all. My parents left my room for three minutes to let me mull over their options. I didn't want to go to the ER or have to sleep in their room, but at the same time I didn't trust myself that night. I had no idea as to whether or not I would compulsively, in a fit of rage and sadness, hurt myself detrimentally. I tried to calm down, and when my parents came back to hear my decision I told them that I wasn't going to do anything harmful to myself and that I would be able to sleep alone that night. When I told them this, I didn't 100 percent believe myself, but I knew that the best way for me to try to relax and clear my head was by being alone. After hearing my response, my parents asked me to promise them that I would hold true to my answer. I hesitantly said yes, and they said good night and reluctantly left the room. I had now just made a promise to my parents, and I have never broken a promise to them before. This actually helped me calm down that night because there was no way that I was going to lie to my parents. I never have and never will.

Later that night, about a half hour after my parents left my room, I decided to try and text AJ one last time. I told her that I was extremely bored and asked her if she wanted to hang out sometime in the next few days. After about 15 minutes, I received a text back. I was ecstatic, yet also scared at the same time. I had no idea what her response was going to be and was very tentative to even read it. I did, however, read the text very soon after I had received it, and much to my dismay and aggravation all she said was "I don't know." I'd had enough of these short, detached texts, so I replied by saying that she needed to tell me what was going on once and for all. I told her that I noticed how the mood in her texts had changed and that she needed to just tell me the truth about her feelings towards me. I went on to explain that I was in no mood whatsoever to play these types of games, and that I would accept any answer she gave me. Five minutes later she responded "I just see us as friends." She had confirmed what

ON THE OUTSIDE LOOKING IN

I had suspected, and I felt so much relief that everything was now out in the open and that my mind would no longer be contemplating all of the different circumstances that might have been taking place. I told her that I was obviously disappointed, but that I still wanted to remain friends, no more, no less. She said she would love to remain friends and still hang out together, just not in a romantic fashion. I agreed, and soon went to sleep feeling a lot better than I did an hour before.

I woke up the next morning feeling exhausted but relieved at the same time. I no longer had to play the awful guessing game. I had a fairly good morning, and my dad and I had a nice conversation about what took place the night before. However, as the day progressed I started to become depressed once again and ended up crying and sleeping in my bed my all day long. I could do nothing but reminisce about all of the great times AJ and I had together. I missed her so much and literally cried every waking hour of the day. This extreme depression ended up lasting more than a week. I would only get out of bed to write and eat, but even then I had a dead affect on my face. I didn't work out or leave the house all week, and my anxiety and obsession about what I ate went through the roof. I also didn't speak to anyone and would barely utter a response if they asked me a question. This was extremely hard for my parents to deal with because they didn't know how they could help me through this, and to be truthful, they couldn't. I had to take this challenge on by myself and hope that the grieving would wear itself out sooner rather than later, even though it had already been more than a week.

A week later, I had been in bed sleeping and crying all day when I received a text from AJ. She told me that she was going to see a movie in one hour and was wondering if I wanted to come along. I jumped at the opportunity and immediately replied with a yes. Even though I knew that she just wanted to be friends, I missed her company so much that there was no way I was going to turn down the invitation, no matter how depressed I was at that point.

We had a good time at the movie, however we didn't talk much before or after. When I was walking her back to her car, I asked her why she decided to break things off. She told me that we were different, which was good, but too different to be in a relationship. This didn't make any sense to me, because I believed that we had a lot in common, including our values, outlook on life, hobbies, sense of humor, etc. She also told me that she didn't think it would work out from the beginning, but she decided to give it a chance anyway. I couldn't help but think that it had something to do with my autism; that she was uncomfortable being around someone with that label. We had great chemistry together and had a blast every time that we hung out. I subsequently told her that I had begun to fall for her, and that I even wrote a poem about her. Looking back on this poem, it is almost shocking to me how innocent, yet naïve I was.

Angela

I've had many people in my life
But no one quite like you
With your persona that makes me naturally high
And your brown eyes of an incredible hue

I make it through the most depressing days
By just imagining your sweet, white smile
You make my problems phase away
And make me giggle like a child

How I stumbled upon you, I will never know
For you are as perfect as perfect can be
Your radiance of beauty emits an everlasting glow
A glow that even Venus could not beat
You're not even worth comparing to any other woman
around
For your essence will truly never be matched

RUSSELL LEHMANN

You walk with such passion, as your feet grace the
ground
While you stand with such splendor that will forever
last

You've turned my life right-side up
A feat that no one has ever accomplished
For before I met you, my life was so rough
You are the angel that fulfilled my wish

You are so very young, yet mature beyond the years
Your self-determination is nothing less than outstanding
You are not afraid to confront your fears
And your passion for life becomes evermore charming
There is a reason your name means angelic
For surely angels had a hand in your creation
Your soul should be forever treasured like a relic
While your heart deserves the most prolonged ovation

So let it be known that you are second to none
You are the epitome of any man's dream
You deserve the best, for you are number one
No woman will ever come close to your sheen

ON THE OUTSIDE LOOKING IN

We soon reached her car, where we said goodbye to one another. As I was walking back to my own car, I started reminiscing about all the great times we'd had while we were dating. Once I got to my car, I got inside and broke down. I was depressed beyond all measures and was crying my eyes out. I started my car and put in Eminem's Recovery album. The feelings that he shares in that CD were so close to mine that it made me break down even more, however it felt good, like I was somehow purging the depression from within me. Listening to the album also helped me release some of the intense anger I was feeling.

I ended up sobbing nonstop throughout the 30 minute drive home. When I pulled into the driveway, I sat in the car for about five minutes, still crying, and then decided to go inside. I went straight to my bedroom and immediately lied down in my bed. The despair that I was feeling was incomprehensible to me, for I was in such mental pain that my whole body began to physically ache with sorrow. For the next few days I did not text AJ. When we did text, it made me feel like she was so close, yet so far away, and that was just too much to bear.

Twelve days later I did in fact text her, wishing her a happy month before her birthday. She never responded back, and she didn't reply to any of my "greeting" texts (i.e. good morning, how are you, etc.) for the rest of that week.

One evening, around 6:15 pm, she sent me a text asking if I had any plans that night. I didn't really feel like going out, especially on such short notice, plus my family and I were just about to start a game of Scrabble. I replied by saying that I was indeed busy that night, and asked her what she was thinking of doing. She told me to not worry about it, which made me even more curious as to what she had in mind. I asked her politely what the harm was in telling me, and she told me that I'm busy anyway, so it doesn't matter. Being very inquisitive, I called her up and asked her why she wouldn't tell me. She sounded irritated, and tersely told me that she was not going to tell me before hanging up on me. Somewhat stunned by her actions, I sent her a text saying that I don't know what the big deal was in telling me, and that I thought her behavior was somewhat childish. I told her that I'll talk to her later if she ever feels like telling me what her idea of hanging out is, especially if she is the one who invited me to hang out. I expected her to respond according to how mature she had seemed when we were dating, but all she said was "……..OK." That was the last time that I ever heard from her.

I texted her the next few days, telling her that I wasn't mad at her in one text and in another asking if she ever wanted to talk again, but to no avail she never responded.

ON THE OUTSIDE LOOKING IN

I started to sink into another deep depression, for I was so afraid of losing all contact with her. I missed her so much, and being at rock bottom, I even asked her if she would give me another chance. However she still didn't reply.

I was feeling no better a few days later, and I decided to write an e-mail to her explaining how I was feeling and where I was coming from.

Hey AJ,

I just wanted to express to you how I am feeling right now. The two and a half weeks you were in my life were by far the happiest, most exciting, and fun time I have ever had. Seriously. I haven't had a true friend since 2001, and you completely filled that void in my life. Before I met you, every day of my life consisted of waking up, working out, watching TV and then going to bed. You opened up a whole new world to me, one that I had never been in before. You gave me a natural high and created such amazing feelings that I had never felt before, and for that I thank you.

I knew throughout the whole time we were "dating" that you didn't want to be in a relationship at that point in time. Still, I was holding on to a thread of hope that sooner or later something might develop between us. When you let me know that you didn't see us as anything more than just friends, it crushed me. I felt like my life had ended. I'm

At the age of 21, I sank into severe depression with
suicidal ideations. I developed anorexia and didn't leave
my house, shower or even change my clothes for fifty-six
straight days. At that point, I voluntarily admitted my-
self to a local inpatient psychiatric hospital.

not trying to make you feel bad, win the sympathy vote, or anything of that kind, because you had every right to express your true feelings and to be totally honest. I am not mad at you nor do I blame you for anything. I just flat out miss you. I stayed in bed crying the whole entire week after you called things off, and I still cry with sorrow every time I think about you, which is daily. I'm not embarrassed telling you that, because it's the truth and I feel no shame behind it.

I want you to try and understand that since I haven't had a friend in over half of my life that I attached myself to you and didn't want to let go. You were what I had been hoping and wishing for for over a decade. I felt pathetic when I texted you and asked you if you could give me one more shot. I was at rock bottom and I didn't know what else to do. I know that you don't have any special feelings towards me, but my mind still doesn't want to believe that.

The main reason behind this e-mail is to let you know that I would still love to be friends with you. You haven't been returning any of my texts, even when I asked you if you ever wanted to talk again. I hope it's not because of that terse text I sent you that one night when you didn't want to tell me what you were thinking of doing when I told you I had plans. I was just so excited to hear from you and when I said that I was busy that night, I knew I blew an opportunity to hang out with you. I was mad at myself and was just so curious as to why you wouldn't tell me what you wanted to do that I became mad at you, too. I apologize if I hurt your feelings or insulted you in anyway.

The bottom line is that I miss hanging out and texting with you. However, as of right now I don't know if I would be able to stand seeing you, for I still haven't gotten over you. When we went to see that movie together, I cried all the way home and went straight to bed. I really don't care if I'm coming off as a pussy because that is how much you meant to me. A real man lets his feelings be known, while a coward hides behind his. I would still like to keep in touch, and as the days progress hopefully see you again.

You're a special person, AJ, and I am not lying when I say that I feel honored to know somebody like you. I hope your moving situation is going smoothly and if you feel like replying, I look forward to hearing back from you.

Best,

Russell

After I had sent this e-mail, I sent her a text asking if she could check her e-mail when she had a chance. She never replied to the e-mail or the text, and it completely crushed my heart, for I knew that I would probably never see her again. That was the last text I ever sent her.

I ended up going in and out of this deep depression for the next 2 ½ months. I would have some good days, but not a day went by without me thinking of AJ and how much happier I was when she was in my life. Once I stopped all communication with AJ, I started to become much less independent in my daily life. Besides the gym, I could not go anywhere by myself (e.g. the grocery store, post office, doctors appointments, etc.). My OCD started to increase drastically and my eating disorder started to quickly become worse and worse. Also, my separation anxiety with regards to my mom began to hinder my daily life. She would work a 12 hour shift (6:00 am – 6:00 pm) about three to four days a week, and on these days I was depressed beyond all measures. The only thing I would do during the days she worked was go to the gym (if I had enough energy) and take naps. On the days she didn't work, it was hard for me to go to the gym because I didn't want to leave her side, and when I didn't go to the gym back then, I would restrict my food intake to the highest extent.

In late August, the depression I was in as a result from losing AJ evolved into a full-blown depression resulting from my agoraphobia and eating disorder. I no longer lamented about AJ, but I was in an even bigger depression than before. All of a sudden, I could no longer leave my house to go to the gym, and I didn't exercise or lift weights for over eight weeks. Besides during recoveries from various surgeries, that was the longest I had ever been inactive in my life. I would sit all day and didn't want to leave the house for any reason at all. During this time is when my eating disorder started to take over my life. I was officially diagnosed with anorexia, and was afraid to put anything that contained calories into my mouth. I started to become feeble and weak, and showed the tale-tell signs of anorexia, such as always being cold, dehydration, dizziness, my hands and feet turning blue, constipation and even having my hair fall out, all at the young age of 21. Every single day I was restricting my intake of food more and more, and actually began to enjoy the feeling of hunger. Somehow I was absolutely convinced that I had gained excess fat since I stopped working out, and was perplexed and highly frustrated at how that came to be, since I was barely eating anything.

Another symptom of anorexia is depression, and added to the depression that I was already suffering from, I hit the lowest point in my life. I began not to care about more and more things every day, and had no interest in doing anything except reading and sleeping. I would take a long nap every single day, and on the days when my mom was at work, I would wash down a Klonopin with a shot glass of NyQuil in order to help me sleep as long as possible. Sleeping was always the best part of the day, because it relieved me from the excruciating mental pain that I was faced with when it came to eating. I cannot describe how awful the anguish was. My obsession about eating combined with my depression literally felt like there was a vice on my brain. The feeling was horrible, and although it's not the best thing to say, I completely understand why people commit suicide when under these conditions.

I soon lost interest in everything in my life except my family. I didn't even begin to think about killing myself because I already truly felt dead inside. I didn't step foot outside the house for over 56 straight days, and I sat on the couch staring into oblivion for most of the day. I also began not to care about my hygiene. I didn't shower this whole time, and before this episode there wasn't a day I did not shower for the previous two years. When I finally did muster up the energy to shower, I would turn off all the lights and try to bathe in complete darkness, for I couldn't bear to see my stomach and the fat that I truly believed I had gained. I still had a muscular six-pack, but that was by far not good enough for me. I couldn't live with any fat on me anywhere, and I expected myself to have the best body in the universe. These were the expectations I put upon myself, and they were destroying my life.

I started to lose about a pound per day, and my condition was starting to become very dangerous. I soon made the very tough decision to be admitted to a residential eating disorder clinic. There were none in Nevada that accepted males so my family and I expanded our search to Utah, Oregon, California and Arizona. We had little luck with finding a quality clinic that excepted Nevada Medicaid in these states, so I decided that although there was a possibility that I would barely be able to see my family, we needed to expand our search country-wide.

After many hours of research, my family and I decided that Rogers Memorial Hospital in Wisconsin was the place best suited to address my needs. They accepted out of state Medicaid, and they had a comprehensive eating disorder program as well as one of the best OCD treatment facilities in the nation. We gave them a call and they administered an application interview over the phone that lasted two hours. After the interview was complete, we were told that they would be calling back within a few days to let us know if they think they could help me. However, it only took one hour for them to call back, and they told us that they spoke with the doctors and were very confident that they could help me out. I had officially been accepted to Rogers Memorial, and my family and I expected to leave for Wisconsin within a matter of days.

We soon found out, however, that Nevada Medicaid needed to reach an agreement with Rogers Memorial in terms of payment. Once we found this out, we called the head of Nevada Medicaid to ask for an update, but she didn't answer the phone and we had to leave a message. She never called us back, even after we had left her two additional messages in the days that followed. My mom ended up calling Rogers Memorial for an update and was shocked when they told her that Nevada Medicaid had refused to play ball with them. Essentially, they were playing my treatment.

When my mom hung up the phone and told me what she had just learned, I fell to the ground and started to sob and scream. I felt like my life was over. I was in such a deep depression and felt that only Rogers Memorial could help me get through it. I continued to lie on the ground crying my eyes out while my mom started to make calls to my therapist and doctor to update them on the situation and ask them if there was anything they could do.

I felt like my life was over. The mental anguish and torment that I was experiencing was so excruciating that I pleaded for God to kill me right then and there. I was going through hell, but as Winston Churchill once said, "When going through hell, keep going."

At this point we were faced with the probability that we would have to start all over in our search for treatment. Throughout the next couple of days we looked at multiple eating disorder and OCD clinics across the nation, but none of them were suited to meet my needs. Rogers Memorial was the perfect fit for me, and my family and I continued to fight for my right to be admitted there.

About a week after we had learned that Nevada Medicaid was refusing to pay for my treatment at Rogers Memorial, we received some good news. It turned out that after Nevada Medicaid started to receive pressure from my doctor, therapist, social worker and even from Senate

Majority Leader Harry Reid's office to have me admitted to Rogers no matter what the cost, they agreed to foot the bill. I was ecstatic, and my parents and I were waiting on one more call from Nevada Medicaid to make sure everything was finalized before we went ahead and booked our plane tickets to Wisconsin.

Nevada Medicaid told us that they would call us the very next day, which would be a Friday, to confirm that the payment had been submitted to Rogers Memorial and that everything was ready to move forward with. All day Friday my parents and I never left our telephone's side, anxiously awaiting the final approval. By 3 p.m. we still had not heard anything, and it was time for my mom to take me to my weekly therapy session. My dad agreed to stay by the phone while we were gone, and so off my mom and I went to see my therapist.

When we arrived at my therapist's office, my mom and I were very excited and relieved that I was finally going to be receiving the help and care that I needed. However, this air of optimism was extinguished as soon as we sat down in my therapist's office. He asked me how I was doing, and when I told him that I was hopeful and excited to finally receive treatment at Rogers Memorial, a perplexed reaction came upon his face. He asked us if we had received a call from Nevada Medicaid that morning, and when we told him no, he appeared increasingly confused. He told us that earlier in the day Nevada Medicaid had called him and told him that they didn't believe I needed inpatient care at the time and that they were going to sign me up for outpatient therapy sessions with a different therapist. They went on to say that I didn't meet the criteria to be admitted to Rogers Memorial, even though I was already approved for admission by Rogers Memorial themselves. They also told my therapist that they would contact my family and I early that day to inform us of their decision, which they did not do.

When I heard this news I was in disbelief. I doubled over the couch I was sitting on and started to cry my eyes out. I was so furious that I was slamming the furniture while yelling out expletives at the top of my lungs. How could a group of people who have never even met me before tell me what the best treatment would be for me? I was nothing but a number to them in the financial game of healthcare and it made me sick to my stomach.

Once my therapist was finished updating me about the circumstances, I remember telling him that I was just going to go ahead and kill myself. Every single day my mental pain was becoming worse and worse, and I knew that my only chance of receiving effective lasting care rested in the hands of Rogers Memorial, and here they were, welcoming me to their facility with open arms while Nevada Medicaid stood blocking the entrance.

At this point in time I had not showered, shaved or changed clothes in 8 weeks. My shirt was stained from wiping away the countless number of tears that I shed, and there was not a day that went by without me sobbing for a good hour. I stopped taking showers altogether because I was too depressed to get out of bed and could not stand to be naked because I was so disgusted with how I thought my body looked. I had not gone to the gym or exercised in months, and any self-esteem that I had left plummeted due to the fact that I was losing all my muscle.

During the latter half of my session with my therapist, my dad called and told us that he had just received a call from Nevada Medicaid. He was in disbelief when they told him that I didn't need inpatient care and that the best course was for me to start seeing another therapist. Medicaid told him that they had received reports from both my psychiatrist and therapist saying that my condition was not severe enough to require inpatient treatment. When my therapist heard this, he threw his arms up in protest. He distinctly told Nevada Medicaid multiple times that the best course of treatment was for me to attend Rogers Memorial. My psychiatrist had also insisted to Medicaid that Rogers Memorial was the best treatment option for me. Nevada Medicaid was lying through their teeth just to save some money, and my therapist was so fed up that he had to cut our session short so that he could make some phone calls to some higher-ups in order to get this whole mess cleared up.

ON THE OUTSIDE LOOKING IN

Over the span of the next few days, we had come to the extremely hard realization that Nevada Medicaid wasn't going to budge in their refusal to pay for my treatment at Rogers Memorial. I was completely and utterly devastated. Every day I thought about killing myself and how sweet it would be to finally rest in peace, and at night, when I would lie in bed, a certain line from Edgar Allan Poe's The Pit and the Pendulum came to mind. "And then there stole into my fancy, like a rich musical note, the thought of what sweet rest there must be in the grave.". The only reason that I didn't go through with it was because I could not bear to put that kind of grief on my family. They had been with me every step of the way when it came to battling all of my disorders and struggles of the last 15 years and there was no way that I was going to give up after all that time spent fighting

Later that week, my therapist assembled a team of doctors, social workers and representatives of Medicaid to try and figure out what the next step would be. We had a conference call with all of them and ultimately came to the decision that since Rogers Memorial was out of the picture, the next best option was for me to admit myself to Northern Nevada Adult Mental Health Services (NNAMHS) for a week to ten days. I reluctantly agreed to this, basically because I was backed up against a wall and had no other options when it came to receiving adequate treatment.

The next morning my parents and I took a tour of the hospital. My parents were impressed with the facility, however I basically made up my mind before the tour even started. It reminded me too much of the hospital in Seattle and I received bad vibes from the nurse who gave us the tour. When we returned home from the tour my parents and I sat down to discuss our options (or lack thereof). I was honest with them and told them that I did not want to admit myself to NNAMHS. I let them know that I could handle my recovery on my own. Even though I hadn't been to the gym in several weeks, I told my parents that I would start working out again the very next day, which I knew deep down was very unlikely. I also told them that I was ready to start leaving the house by myself to run errands, go to doctor's appointments, etc. Looking back on this conversation now, there was no doubt that I was in a form of denial.

After a lengthy talk, my parents made me come to my senses and agree to admit myself to NNAMHS. Since I was voluntarily admitting myself, I could also discharge myself at any point in time for any reason. With this in mind, I started to pack for my stay, which was to begin the next day.

Prior to me being admitted, my family and I had made arrangements to meet with the hospital's dietician in order to come up with a food plan for me. During the tour of the hospital we had explained to the nurse that I had an eating disorder and told him how wary I was of eating the food the hospital would be providing. I was already extremely self-conscious about the way I looked because I hadn't exercised in so long, and I dreaded being served food every day without being able to have a say about what I ate. I was used to eating the same exact things every single day at home and I wasn't going to be allowed to bring any food with me. He eased our worries when he told us that their dietician would be able to order the foods for me that I usually ate at home.

I walked into NNAMHS with my mom at around 12pm with bags in hand. We met with the head nurse who we had spoken to on the phone beforehand and she let us know that we would be meeting the dietician later in the day. I was expecting that my mom was going to be able to stay with me for a short amount of time while I got situated in my room and used to my surroundings. However, about twenty minutes after we arrived, they told us that it was time for me to do my intake and that my mom wasn't going to be able to accompany me. They let me say goodbye to my mom, which I did with tears flowing down my cheeks, and then ushered me into the intake office.

While I was filling out all the required forms, the staff was going through all my bags to make sure I didn't have anything dangerous. They ended up taking from me my laptop (which they previously said I could bring in so I could write my poetry), my MP3 player, my phone, all of the shorts that I packed (because they had strings in them), my shoes (because of the laces), and all of my toiletries (they provided me with my own toothbrush and toothpaste). The only thing that I was able to take back with me to my room was a book I brought: "Wieland", an 18th century novel by Charles Brockden Brown.

I felt as if the hospital lured me into admitting myself by telling me everything I wanted to hear in my visit prior to my admittance, for once my intake was complete they went back on their word with regards to almost everything.

For the next three hours after my intake was complete, I stayed in my bed, curled up in a ball and crying, feeling betrayed and regretful. I wanted to be anywhere else but there.

I soon became extremely hungry and was able to compose myself for a short amount of time to ask one of the staff members if I could get a granola bar out of my suitcase. They told me that everything I brought in with me wasn't allowed, so instead they offered me a pack of graham crackers. I reluctantly took them, but after reading the nutrition facts, I decided not to eat them because they had trans fat in them. As the dietician told me my diet would be accommodated, this was another dagger in my heart and soul.

After four hours of staying in what felt like a prison, it was time to head down to the cafeteria for dinner. My eyes red from crying, I begrudgingly got out of my bed and slipped on the sandals they provided for my feet. I was beyond hungry and was hoping that there would be something in the cafeteria that I would be willing to eat. Once we got down to where the food was, I saw that they were serving hot dogs, macaroni salad and broccoli. Another dagger. I felt like having a meltdown and was becoming increasingly resentful for the way I was lead on by the dietician and staff.

I ended up eating a whole plate of plain broccoli and nothing else. Not thirty minutes after I finished eating I was hungry once again. I ended up sitting in my dark room (there was no light switch, and I was unable to open the blinds as they were locked behind plexiglass) crying until my parents showed up during visitors hours, about two hours later.

I cried the whole time I was with my parents and begged them not to leave once visiting hours were up. When they very reluctantly did so (the staff had to force them out), I immediately went to bed, hoping that the next day would be much better. As it was only 8:00pm, the hospital was still very noisy and I went to the front desk to ask for my earplugs that I had brought. When they refused to give them to me, saying that I needed a doctor's note, I was beyond mad and I felt like my freedom was being taken away from me little by little. Nevertheless, I went to bed

RUSSELL LEHMANN

and tried to fall asleep, which took an incredible length of time.

The next morning I was awoken by a knock at my door at 6:00am. At 6:30am we went down to the cafeteria for breakfast, and to my dismay I found them serving French toast and scrambled eggs. I had one scoop of scrambled eggs and that was it. After I was done eating, which took about 45 seconds, I went back to my room and started balling. I was the hungriest I had ever been, and for the next nine hours I didn't eat a single thing, which was by far the longest I had gone without eating during the day. I had decided that I could not stay here any longer, and throughout the day I called my parents multiple times to let them know the terrible condition I was in and to make sure that they were coming during visiting hours. At this point I had only been in this hospital for a little over half a day, and what was left of my well being prior to my stay here had already been greatly diminished.

With the exception of getting up to call my parents every hour, I stayed in my room the whole day. Multiple times staff members would knock on my door and ask me if I wanted to participate in Jazzercise or play games with the other patients. I sternly declined every time and I was becoming increasingly frustrated with their persistence. When I was first admitted, the head administrator specifically told my parents and I that I would not have to participate in anything that I didn't want to. Yet another sign that we were led on.

At one point one of the staff members came into my room and sternly told me that I needed to start participating in the group events. Holding back tears, I told her that I wasn't up for it, for I was too depressed. After hearing this, she immediately started to scold me about how I'm not taking any initiative in my recovery. What she said had infuriated me. Not only had I taken the initiative to start my recovery by voluntarily admitting myself to the hospital, but I placed my trust in those operating the conditions of the hospital. The main reason I stayed inside my room all day was because the environment of the hospital was not at all conducive to my recovery. Many of the patients that were there were admitted by the order of a court because they were addicted to drugs and/or alcohol, while the others were senior citizens who had a plethora of severe mental illnesses. Although I had and have absolutely nothing against these patients, for they were battling their demons just as I was battling mine, it was clear to me that this was not the healing, therapeutic environment my mind so desperately craved.

To give you an example of how chaotic the hospital was, there was one woman who would routinely take off all her clothes and run around naked. She thought that she could climb walls whenever she didn't have her clothes on, and attempted to do so every chance she got. There was also an elderly man who would pull down his pants and start going to the bathroom anywhere that he felt the urge to do so. Again, I am not at all trying to stigmatize or put down those with other disorders or hardships in their lives, I am just letting you know how the atmosphere of the hospital was not at all beneficiary to the recovery of a quiet guy with autism.

After hearing what the staff member just said, I told her that I have autism, and that I was not at all comfortable participating in group events. She told me that I needed to participate anyway because it would ultimately help my recovery. I replied back by saying that she obviously hadn't worked with autistic individuals before, because when someone has autism, the last thing you want to do is force them into a chaotic, foreign environment that has an extremely high chance of triggering sensory overload. After she heard this, she got extremely defensive and started to literally yell at me, telling me that I knew nothing about her and that she had indeed worked with autistic children for many years. Having someone who felt like they needed to defend themselves and doing so by yelling at me was definitely the last thing that I needed. How she thought this was beneficial to me I have no idea. After she was done going off on her tangent, I calmly replied that she must not have been very helpful to those autistic children and told her that if she wasn't going to talk to me like an adult, then she needed to leave my room immediately.

ON THE OUTSIDE LOOKING IN

She said something unintelligibly under her breath and stormed out of my room. I was at a total loss for what had just happened, and I couldn't believe that an adult in her line of work could act so immature. At this point I had lost any of the remaining hope I had within me.

About five minutes after she left my room, I got up out of my bed to go to the bathroom, and as I entered the hallway, I found, much to my disgust, the staffer divulging everything that had just taken place inside my private room to another staffer, all the while laughing. Seeing this put me over the top. I walked over to her and said "Seriously?! You're making chitchat out of something that just took place behind closed doors?! You should be ashamed of yourself! I don't know how the hell you were ever allowed into this profession and I sure as hell hope you aren't in it for much longer!" She stared at me blankly the whole time I said this and I subsequently went back into my room and slammed the door behind me.

I stayed in my room sobbing for the next five hours, until my parents came during visiting hours. At one point, I had cried so much that there were no more tears left for me to shed. I was immensely depressed, and I still shudder when I think about the state of mind I was in that whole day. I felt worse than at any other point in my life, and all I simply wanted was to die.

When visiting hours started approaching I was listening very carefully to what was going on in the hallway outside my room where the front desk was. I was anxiously waiting to hear that my parents had arrived, and I soon rejoiced when I did indeed hear these words. I waited for one of the staff members to come into my room and let me know that I had visitors, but after ten minutes, no one had come in. I finally went out into the hallway and up to the front desk and asked one of the staff members if my parents had arrived yet. The main doctor that was handling my medications overheard me ask this and came over to tell me that my parents were not there. I told him that I heard one of the staffers announce their arrival, but he kept telling me that I was wrong. "I have been standing here for the last 30 minutes and I haven't heard anything" he said. I knew he was lying through his teeth just because he was mad at me for not participating in the group events. He then immediately asked me if I was going to be participating in that evening's events, and when I sternly told him no and that I was absolutely positive that I heard someone say that my parents had arrived, he nonchalantly shrugged and said "You're wrong. You didn't hear a thing. If you are not going to be participating in tonight's group events then I suggest you go back into your room" and turned his back on me and walked away. I was beyond furious. I was just about to cuss him out when I decided to make the better decision to ask a staff member if my parents had arrived, and she immediately told me that yes, they arrived about 20 minutes ago and were waiting for me in the conference room.

Once I went into the conference room and laid my eyes on my parents I completely broke down. I felt like I hadn't seen them in years and I felt so much more comfortable just seeing their faces. I told them that I couldn't stay at the hospital any longer, and as I told them this I felt extremely disappointed with myself. I felt like I was letting myself and my parents down because this hospital was the only resource we had and I felt like I was giving up on my recovery. Yet, looking back, I am incensed that this hospital was indeed the only option available to me. A hospital that lied to me, yelled at me and made fun of me. A hospital that did not provide a single accommodation to a struggling individual with autism. A hospital that contributed to the ultimate deterioration of my mental health and well being.

After apologizing to my parents multiple times, they asked me if I could try and stay here for at least another day just so I could be observed as I was changing medications. I told them that I really wished I could and that I wanted to be strong for them but that I felt like I was in a prison in all aspects. Even as my parents and I were having our discussion, there was a nurse holding the door open to the conference room we were in to keep an eye on us.

As my parents and I continued our conversation, we went over the pros and the cons of discharging me from the hospital. In the end I decided, with the support of my parents, to discharge myself from the hospital. As I was walking out the front doors, I felt an intense mix of emotions. I felt free and extremely happy, however I also knew that I was still in the middle of the worst depression of my life and I didn't know how the choice of discharging myself from the hospital would affect me in the long run.

The first evening I spent back at home was extremely comforting. I was very happy, but this happiness was much different than what I usually feel. I was glad to be home, but I felt like this joy was just a mask. Deep down, I still felt dead inside, and I knew that once I woke up the next morning the happiness that I did feel at that point in time would be gone. I tried to stay in the moment and only think about the present, but my OCD soon conquered that attempt.

I was once again back at square one, however I can tell you that I felt much comfort, and, for the first time in weeks, I had a reason to be happy and grateful due to being back in my own home. That first night back in my own bed I was physically and mentally spent due to the previous 30 hours, however I still remember how special it was to smile as I drifted off into a much needed sleep. I can't tell you how comforting it felt to feel the emotions behind a smile that I had come to forget about. Yet, when

ON THE OUTSIDE LOOKING IN

I woke up the next morning, as I expected, reality hit me like a brick when I realized I was still at rock bottom, with a long way to go before even beginning to see any light.

The two weeks following my discharge from the hospital were by far the worst in my life. I was going through extreme withdrawals from stopping all of my medications at once while in the hospital, and every day I sunk deeper and deeper into my depression. During these two weeks I took my first shower in close to 2 months and changed out of the clothes I had been wearing that entire time. Every day I would wake up, lie on the sofa and watch TV for four to five hours, take a two to three hour nap, wake up and then watch TV for the rest of the day. I was barely eating anything, and I had lost about 30 pounds, my weight being at 150lbs (I'm just under 6'2").

Having been off my usual medications for a couple days at this point, I was now only taking Cymbalta, which the doctor at NNAMHS put me on. I was told that it could take two to three weeks for the medicine to kick in, but I was hopeful that I would feel some relief much sooner than that. Unfortunately, I didn't feel any relief at all, and every day my OCD, depression and anxiety was increasing tenfold. I couldn't stand being away from my mom, and whenever she left the house, either to run errands or go to work, I would have the most agonizing thoughts about her. I would lie in bed crying my eyes out as I couldn't help but think that she would die in a car crash or in some other manner. These intrusive thoughts were so real to me that I would even be planning what I would wear to her funeral and how I would be acting in the stages of grief that I would be going through. My brain literally felt like it was crumbling to pieces, and my only relief from this excruciating mental pain was to fantasize about how peaceful it would be to once and for all be lowered into my grave.

After about a week of going through this tremendous mental agony, I broke down in front of my mom when she got home from work one night. She held me in her arms, and I knew she could tell that I was literally, LITERALLY dying inside. After crying in her arms for over an hour, she suggested that I go back onto Anafranil, a tricyclic antidepressant that also reduces the symptoms of OCD. I was taking Anafranil before I was admitted to NNAMHS, but the doctor there took me off of it. I agreed with my mother's proposal to start taking the medication again, and this decision ended up being a major turning point in my recovery.

For the next four days, my OCD and the horrible thoughts that accompanied it slowly started to dissipate. I was still just lying in bed all day, but I knew that I would soon be able to start pushing myself towards my goal, which was to defeat my depression, OCD, anxiety and my eating disorder all together.

About ten days after I started back on the Anafranil, I decided to try and go workout at the gym. It had been 57 days since I last worked out, by far the longest I had ever gone in my life. Ever since I had been in my deep depression, I was too afraid to even walk across the street to get the mail, so setting my sights on driving to the gym and going inside by myself was immense.

I was able to fill my water bottle up, and put on my workout clothes, but when the time came to walk out the front door I was feeling so overwhelmed that I collapsed. I sat on the kitchen floor and cried for about 30 minutes. I wanted to go so bad, but I just didn't have it in me. I knew that if I did go, even if I only went inside for five minutes, I would feel tremendously accomplished, but the mental strength just wasn't there. I felt like I let myself down and that I was giving up, but I knew that I would keep trying until I accomplished my goal.

A week passed before I tried going to the gym again, and I told myself that this time nothing was going to get in the way of me achieving my goals. I took it step by step. I planned on driving to the gym, and if I didn't feel like I could go in, at least I left the house by myself. I got all ready to go, and this time I put my headphones on and listened to motivating music (specifically "'Till I Collapse" by Eminem) to give me that extra push I needed. I was able to walk out the front door, get into my car and drive to the gym. I knew I had already accomplished a huge feat, but I was hungry for more. When I parked my car, I immediately jumped out and went inside without thinking, because idle thoughts are detrimental to me in times like these. I only worked out for about 30 minutes, but after I walked out of the gym and got into my car I felt like I had just climbed Mt. Everest. I was extremely ecstatic and proud of myself. I was screaming and hollering at the top of my lungs, knowing that I had just conquered the most impossible challenge I had ever been faced with. However, I knew that there was still a tremendous amount of work to be done, but I knew that after what I had accomplished that morning, nothing was going to hold me back from returning to that happy, funny, energetic Russell I had been missing for so long.

That week I went to the gym four days in a row, and I felt unstoppable. I never turned back and I started working out on a regular basis once again. I was even able to go out on a date later that month.

I ended up fully recovering from my depression by the end of that year, 2012. I was still struggling with my eating disorder, OCD and anxiety, however the main obstacle that was previously in my path I had cleared. Suffice to say that I was very much looking forward to the new year of 2013, a fresh start.

2013-2014

The next two years provided ample life experiences for me that ultimately led to immense personal growth. I fell in love for the first time (while also suffering my worst heartbreak), moved out on my own successfully, made my first friend in over 10 years, acquired my very first job and became involved in my first long-term relationship with a wonderful woman who I'm still friends with to this day.

Suffice to say that I was determined during these two years to make up for all the experiences I had missed out on during my teenage years. Several enlightening, eye-opening and just plain fun events occurred during this time, however I'm still, to this day, a novice when it comes to the art of social interaction.

In late 2014, I was satisfied with all that I had accomplished with regards to my social life, however this left me wanting something more. Something substantive, profound, meaningful. I was in search of something that would enrich my soul, and nurture the tenacious ambition that has always been a significant part of who I am.

During the last few months of 2014, I hit another rough spot and ultimately lost contact with the outside world again. Aside from going to the gym every morning, I stayed inside my house as much as possible, which became excruciatingly lonely, for at this time I was living by myself. I remember many days where, during the late afternoon, I would curl up into a ball on the carpet and stay there well into the night, all the while crying and questioning my existence. This, however, proved to be the biggest blessing in disguise.

In the midst of this loneliness, I felt as though I was at rock bottom again. Yet, it occurred to me that being at rock bottom left me with a clean slate, a solid foundation to build whatever my heart desired. So with this, I took it upon myself to discover my true being. I dreamed, I philosophized, I delved into the depths of my soul. I soon found out what my heart, body and mind yearned for, and subsequently constructed a bulletproof plan to make my goals come to fruition. I had finally discovered the meaning of my existence.

2015-2016

In early 2015 it was clear to me that I had a moral obligation to start using my voice on a larger scale, for throughout all the painful experiences in my life, I had learned many valuable lessons and gained tremendous insight, and I did not feel right keeping these to myself. I had to start sharing them with the world.

With this in mind, I decided to take my shot at public speaking, with the intent to make it my career. After slowly putting together different aspects of my career blueprint, I gave my first official speech on October 23, 2015 at a fundraiser for the Autism Coalition of Nevada in front of about 100 people. I received a standing ovation and mingled with the audience for about an hour afterwards, many of whom believed I was already a professional speaker and were astonished to find out that I had just given my very first speech.

The natural high I felt during this event was unexplainable. My words produced a roomful of emotions, from tears of hope to waves of inspiration. After the event that night, as I was lying in bed, I knew I was on my way, and the next morning I woke up hungry for more.

A few months later I had the amazing opportunity to present at a nationwide disability conference in Washington D.C., and as one member of the audience told me afterwards, I "brought down the house". Since then my speaking career has taken off like a rocket, but not without endless dedication, practice, research, marketing and commitment. At times my relentless drive and ambition affects my well-being, but thankfully I have an amazing support system who calls me out when they see that I'm pushing myself too hard.

2017

2017 was my first full calendar year of speaking, and it totally exceeded my expectations. I traveled to over 25 cities, in all corners of the country, keynoting national conferences, lecturing at universities, facilitating first-responder trainings, and educating the masses.

Perhaps the most prominent and profound event that happened during my extensive travels this year was meeting a man by the name of David. He works for American Airlines, and this man not only saved my day, flight and speech, but also my long-term well-being. To give you the full effect of the story, I will start from the beginning.

Due to my life becoming more and more busy, my meltdowns have been occurring more frequently lately, and I'm finding it somewhat difficult to come to terms with the stern realization that these tumultuous, demoralizing meltdowns may always be a significant part of my life.

Two of these meltdowns happened in 2017 in public, both of them at airports, on back-to-back days nonetheless. The first day I was on my way to Michigan to keynote a state conference. The jet ended up sitting on the tarmac for over an hour, and as I finally arrived at my first layover in Salt Lake City I wasn't surprised that I had missed my connection. However what did surprise me was that the earliest I was going to be able to make it to Michigan was the following day at noon, far passed the time I was scheduled to give my keynote that day. I relayed this to the conference scheduling team, hoping they could reschedule my speech, however they told me that unfortunately that was not going to be possible, and to head back home to Reno. I was devastated, to put it mildly. As an individual on the spectrum, I take comfort in having an absolutely solid schedule and itinerary, and the slightest change can dissolve my entire well-being. You could compare this to a circuit board: one faulty connection can blackout the entire system.

Aside from the drastic change in plans, I was also extremely disappointed and discouraged at missing the opportunity to present at a statewide conference, something that I was very much looking forward to. All these factors resulted in me beginning to experience a meltdown at the Salt Lake airport. To add to this, I soon found out that my checked bag was on its way to Michigan without me, and that I would have to wait at the airport for over 7 hours in order to catch the next plane back home to Reno.

Suffice to say...I lost it. There's honestly no other way to describe it. I stumbled to a quiet corner of the airport and sat down, sobbing, shaking, and rocking back and forth. I ended up staying in that same exact spot for the next 7 hours, half of that time still crying, disassociating and losing touch with my physical body, all the while feeling like I was trapped in a living hell, which I was. The mental pain and torment I was experiencing was indescribable. Passersby would stare at me with confused and bewildered looks, and not once did I receive the simplest sign of compassion, such as a small smile or a head nod. Looking back, this was perhaps the most disturbing and disheartening aspect of this whole incident: the complete and utter lack of compassion that I encountered.

All in all I finally made it back home to Reno at 2am, traumatized, exhausted and depleted. Later the next day, however, I was to fly out to Cincinnati for another keynote. I was supposed to fly to Cincinnati straight from Michigan, but obviously I never made it to Michigan, so I had to rebook my flight.

Before I left for the airport, I made sure to take all the necessary precautions, such as checking to see if the flight was on time, etc. Everything seemed to be a go. Yet, once again, after I boarded the plane, we were again stuck on the tarmac for over an hour. Trying to hold myself together, I asked the flight attendant if there was any chance of making my connection in Chicago. Her answer was probably not, and that I may have to stay overnight in Chicago and catch a flight to Cincinnati the next morning. I began to have a panic attack, along with a meltdown, due to the drastic change in schedule yet again, and began experiencing sensory overload due to the voices of all the angry passengers asking what the holdup was. I couldn't believe this was happening for a second straight day!

Luckily, I was able to tell one of the crew members that I have autism, was beginning to experience a meltdown, and needed to get off the plane, however she very sternly told me that was not going to be possible and to have a seat. This resulted in me panicking even more, and actually punching the lavatory door while screaming expletives at the top of my lungs. That same crew member then turned around and said "Sir, you're going to have to leave the plane", with which I let out a big sarcastic "Thank You!" One of the few times punching and cussing worked out in my favor!

So I grabbed my bags and exited the aircraft, and found an empty ticket counter to sit behind. This is when I succumbed to the worst meltdown of my life. I curled up into a ball, tears were pouring out of my eyes, all my muscles convulsing at a rapid pace as I began to sweat profusely, hyperventilating, while my body shook in terror. I wanted to go home, to say the least.

This time, however, instead of being confronted with stares from people around me like I was the previous day, an airline employee saw that I was in distress and calmly approached me. I wrote a FaceBook post about this experience the following morning:

 Russell Lehmann: Speaker, Author, Advocate is 😌 feeling eternally grateful with **Russell Lehmann** at **Reno-Tahoe International Airport.**

Jun 4, 2017 at 8:45 AM · Reno, Nevada · 🌐

This is David. He works for **American Airlines**. I will never forget this man for as long as I live.

After having my flight delayed and missing my connection for the second time in two days, I succumbed to the worst meltdown of my life at the **Reno-Tahoe International Airport**. He happened to find me curled up behind a vacant ticket counter.

I was crying my eyes out, rocking back and forth as my muscles convulsed at a rapid pace. Sweating profusely, I was hyperventilating while my body shook in terror.

David calmly approached me, and with the utmost compassion, he asked me what was wrong. I was barely able to get any words out. I believe I mumbled the words "I don't know. I can't think, I have autism." He crouched down beside me and let me know that there was still a way I could get to Cincinnati late that night, therefore making it possible for me to give my speech the next day.

During a time of indescribable mental torment and anguish, this man showed me compassion. This man showed that he cared. Hell, he even offered to buy me a slice of pizza for lunch!

David offered to reroute my flight, and he gave me some time to think about it, for I told him that I was afraid of exacerbating my symptoms by boarding another flight, i.e. a tightly enclosed space filled with vast amounts of stimuli.

After about 10 minutes, David approached me again, this time accompanied by the pilot of the plane I had the choice of boarding. David had notified the pilot, along with the entire crew, of my situation, and he took it upon himself to clear out a whole row of seats so that I would be able to have space to myself during the flight. The pilot was also incredibly kind, reminding me that what I was experiencing only added validity to the message I spread. To the lives I touch.

I ended up deciding to board the flight. I was the very first to board, and David walked onto the plane with me, introducing me to the flight crew one by one. I was still shaking and crying, but this time I was crying tears of thankfulness. If it hadn't been for David, I would not have gotten on that plane.

This post isn't about autism. It's about doing the right thing. About being a good person. About accepting others and reaching out your hand to someone in need, even if they are a total stranger.

This post spread like wildfire, soon going viral with the hashtag #BeLikeDavid and being featured in countless media outlets such as USA Today, Yahoo! News, American Airlines' national newsletter, Autism Speaks and NPR, with the story even being archived for eternity in the Library of Congress!

To this day, the story has reached over 20 million people all around the world, and leading to the much deserved recognition of David's actions and him being nominated for numerous awards in customer service.

A day after my disheartening experience in Salt Lake City, David restored my faith in humanity. He showed me that acceptance and compassion are out there, and perhaps the best part about this whole experience, is that it encouraged millions of people around the world to be more like David. David gave us all a glimpse into what we as a society are capable of when we look out for one another.

ON THE OUTSIDE LOOKING IN

Later in 2017, in December, I took a tremendous risk and decided to go on a much needed vacation, all by myself, to Europe nonetheless!

I went into the venture with no expectations. I had the outlook that even if the whole trip was a disaster, once I returned home I would still be able to say that I did it: I will have gone to Europe alone, and I did not let my disability and daily challenges stand in the way of doing what I wanted.

And so I went, and much to my surprise, it was the best 10 days of my life. I traveled to Spain, France, Monaco and Italy, each day being present in the moment and not having any expectations other than to enjoy the ride.

Sure, there were some very difficult times when I would breakdown in my room or be hit with immense anxiety and/or depression, but I persevered like I always do, and accepted my emotions as part of the human experience.

2018

As stated, I currently travel to all corners of the country spreading my message of hope, inspiration, awareness and understanding, not just for those with disabilities, but for the general population as well.

Some people see all the success I have had and assume that I no longer struggle, but I do. Vehemently at times. Every single day is a fight, and I fight not because I want to, but because I'm capable. I find it my moral obligation to do so. If I'm given a capability I am going to utilize it, and the best thing about the will to fight is that it is in each and every one of us. Sure I get tired, I get worn down, I get discouraged. I lose a Hell of a lot of battles, but what matters is that I always come back to win the wars.

Don't let my progress fool you. I still have autism, I still suffer from severe depressive episodes, I continue to have bouts of incapacitating anxiety, every day I fight a battle with my brain in order to maintain control over my OCD, and I still struggle with my eating disorder. I will always have these obstacles, and they will always be a significant part of who I am. As the saying goes, "Life does not get easier, you just get stronger".

I sincerely hope that reading my story has made you realize what massive potential resides within each and every one of us, no matter who we are, what we have been through or what we are going through. Success is not random. Every single one of us has the capability to achieve whatever we desire in this world.

In closing, yes, I may have a disability, but I refuse to let my disability have me. It used to have me, but it never will again, and it may grab me by the foot sometimes, but I always manage to shake free. Always.

I am pleased to be a voice for the unheard, for I know how challenging and frustrating it is to go unnoticed. I give hope to families and parents who are concerned with their child's future, just as my parents once were. I let kids who are struggling with anything, know that no matter how cliché it sounds, life does get better, it may not get easier, but it does get better, the key is you just have to believe it will. I can't let all the pain and agony I've been through, and still continue to go through, to be for nothing. I have to use these experiences, and the lessons I've learned from them, to help others.

To put it simply, that is my goal in life, to help others.

RUSSELL LEHMANN

"Simple pleasures, the last refuge
Of the complex"
~Oscar Wilde

RUSSELL LEHMANN

RUSSELL LEHMANN

RUSSELL LEHMANN

My Thoughts On

Being Different

A lot of kids out there are ashamed of being different, and understandably so. It's difficult when you don't fit in with the crowd, especially as a vulnerable youth. I have come to find, however, that being different is an amazing blessing in disguise. Being different, at its core, simply means that you are a catalyst for change in the future, and guess what? If you don't fit in, that means you stand out. You stand out due to your unique qualities while also helping to add diversity to the world. How boring would it be if we were all the same? Those who are "different" from the majority of the population help our society to not stagnate, while continuously helping our communities to evolve and accept other viewpoints and perspectives.

Are you weird? I sure am. But I'll tell you a secret: all the best people are!

Meltdowns

Due to my life becoming increasingly busier, my melt-downs have been occurring more frequently lately, and I'm finding it somewhat difficult to come to terms with the stern realization that these tumultuous, demoralizing meltdowns may always be a significant part of my life.

Taking a realistic approach about this ongoing struggle in my life helps me to battle it more effectively. Instead of avoiding this significant demon of mine, and pretend-ing it is not there like I have done in the past, I now look it in the eyes and recognize the essence of this demon: a testament to the mental strength I have acquired over the years. Think of this video game analogy:

The further you progress in a video game, and the higher the level that you're on, the game becomes increas-ingly difficult. It's an indication that you have progressed in the game, and that you need more of a challenge in order for you to want to keep playing.

I find the same thing when it comes to my difficult episodes such as meltdowns. Although I abhor the mental pain and anguish it brings upon me, I have to consciously remind myself during these struggles that this is the time

ON THE OUTSIDE LOOKING IN

I show what I'm made of, how much stronger I've become since my last episode.

The take away is to take pride in having these challenges in your life, and to always remember that the heaviest burdens are only placed upon the shoulders of those strong enough to carry them. Having challenges in life is no accident. You were chosen to face them!

Emotions

A lesson that I have just recently come upon, and one that I still find very difficult to master, is learning how to handle my emotions. Emotions are one of the most powerful components in this world, and oftentimes they tend to hold us back from going after what we truly desire. I have learned, through trial and error, to not let my emotions dictate my actions. In order to do this, we must first learn to recognize our feelings, and then control them, or else they will control us.

We've all been there. Days when you are too depressed to even get out of bed. Nights when you are invited out but don't know too many people who will be there, so you decide to bail. Opportunities that await you, but your fear of failure and lack of self-confidence tell you to just wait for the next opportunity instead.

Every time we let our emotions dictate how we live, they grow a little bit stronger, and we become just a little more obedient to them. As I said before, emotions are vastly powerful forces of nature. It will take time to learn how to properly control them, and when I say properly, I mean in a healthy manner.

ON THE OUTSIDE LOOKING IN

The last thing you want to do is suppress or hide your emotions, for they will fester inside of you and continue to grow stronger. That is why I mentioned that we must first recognize our feelings before we control them. The biggest mistake we can make is pretending to not feel our emotions. We must give our emotions the respect they deserve, for they are formidable opponents. By doing so, and recognizing our emotions, we become aware. Aware of what our bodies are feeling and cognizant of how to appropriately respond.

Overcoming Adversity

Life is hard, for everybody. And yes, although it is an absolute truth that some individuals and families have it harder than others, the fact is that everybody has moments in their life where they are tested, where they are pushed into a corner with seemingly no way out. Now personally, for me, these are the moments I live for. This is my chance, this is your chance! Are we going to just sit in the corner and give up, or are we going to get up, get up to prove people wrong, prove the world wrong?

Succumb or overcome, the choice is up to us, and guess what? The comeback is, and will always be, stronger than the setback!

We must learn to look at our lives as a story that we are fortunate enough to be the authors of. We may go through some bad chapters, but that doesn't mean the whole book is going to be bad! The pen is in our hand and the ending to our story has not been written yet, so are we going to write a story that will make others feel sorry for us when they read it, or are we going to write a comeback story? A story of beating the odds, of overcoming adversity while staring directly into the face of what seems likes insurmountable trials and tribulations. The pen is in our hands and we all have the power to end our story however we choose to, so ask yourself: How will I end mine?

Understand that the heaviest burdens in life are only put upon those strong enough to carry them. Instead of asking yourself "Why me?" Ask yourself, "Why not me?"

When you get tested in life, embrace it. Similar to when you are taking a test in school, when life administers a test you learn what you are capable of and what improvements you can make in order to fulfill your full potential.

Stepping Out of Your Comfort Zone

I think we all know that rarely does anything worthwhile occur inside of your comfort zone. The magic happens once we take that first step outside of our comfort zone. Not only do we reap the benefits of whatever risks we take, but we also build up our confidence and self-esteem, which will immediately carry over into your everyday life. On top of this, when we continually subject ourselves to new environments, circumstances, experiences and stimuli, our brains literally form new synaptic connections. It's safe to say that embracing change is a great workout for the brain. It becomes stronger, more efficient and is better adept at handling stressful situations.

Embracing change and stepping outside of your comfort zone is scary. It definitely takes courage. Some people think that courage is not having fear, but I have to disagree. Courage is all about having a tremendous amount of fear, but deciding to face it anyway.

Aristotle, on the other hand, believed that courage was a virtue, a disposition. Something that others have and that some don't, but I have to disagree with that assumption as well! Everybody has courage, the same exact amount. Courage is not something that some people are born with and others aren't. It's just whether or not we choose to use our courage. It's all about choice, about taking risks, and accepting that you may very well fail in your efforts.

RUSSELL LEHMANN

Failure

While on the subject of failure, it is perhaps one of the biggest fears known to man. There is immense pressure from society to not fail in each and every aspect of our lives, as if we are machines capable of succeeding in everything we desire to do. Few people realize, however, that failure is completely natural. In fact, it plays a significant and vital role in who we are as individuals. My take? Society should not be shunning failure, but rather applauding those who fail for using their courage to go against the grain.

We usually fail before we succeed, so think of failure as being halfway there!

Bottom line: Failure is not something we should be afraid of. Rather, we should be embracing our failures, for they are the biggest motivators out there! If we were to never fail, we would never realize the utter strength and perseverance that resides within each and every one of us, and we would never find out we are truly capable in this world. As I always say, you have to look at failures as trampolines: You're going to fall, but you will bounce back better because of it!

Being Aware
Acceptance - understanding and awareness

If you've noticed the national dialogue about autism and other disabilities has shifted somewhat over the past couple of years, from seeking awareness to now seeking acceptance, but to be honest I think we're getting ahead of ourselves here, for we are still a long way away from achieving full awareness within society. Think about it: How can society ever come to accept something that it doesn't fully understand or isn't fully aware of?

This is why I will always be on a mission to spread absolute, 100% transparent awareness about what I struggle with. Why I completely bare my soul on social media, in my speeches and in my books. I do this in order to further the possibility of acceptance down the road, not just for me, not just for those with autism, not just for those with disabilities. I want everyone, every, single person on this planet to be accepted for who they are and for us as a society and as a community to understand and realize that there is a lot of pain in this world. A LOT. Be compassionate to one another. Be understanding. We are all in this together, and if it's just 2 things we all have in common it's that we are all human, and that we all struggle at times.

What I'm describing falls under the ultimate rule of humanity, a rule that has seem to gradually fallen on deaf ears recently, the Golden Rule, or Law of Reciprocity, a maxim in countless religions and cultures all over the world: "Do unto others, as you would have them do unto you".

Passion

Passion is the catalyst behind our drive to perform at the best of our ability. I always preach about following your heart, for you truly have a greater chance of success if you follow whatever your heart leads you into, and that is because you are passionate it.

If you are truly passionate about your job, you'll never work a day in your life. If you are sincerely passionate about another person, you'll find out the true meaning of love, and not just romantic love, but platonic love as well. If you are genuinely passionate about yourself and all that you are, you will begin to see the world in a whole new light, and will come to love yourself unconditionally.

There may not be a more powerful engine to propel us towards are dreams than passion.

RUSSELL LEHMANN

Being your own best friend

After everything I have been through, I have learned the secret to being able to bounce back after life throws you against the wall, and that secret is to be your own best friend. Like it or not, you're going to be stuck with yourself for the rest of your life, so you might as well put in the effort to get to know yourself, and learn to appreciate and love who you are deep down inside.

Additionally, throughout our lives there is only one person we can completely and entirely count on no matter the circumstances, and that lone person is ourselves.

Don't forget about yourself. Pay attention to what your body is telling you. Listen to your heart, your soul, your mind. Only then will you begin to understand who you are, and what you can achieve. All the answers are within YOU. As the Romantic poet Novalis once wrote. "The path of mystery leads inwards".

And if you are ever wondering what you can hold on to during those difficult times, the answer is yourself. Literally. Give yourself a hug.

Perseverance

Perseverance has been a major theme of my life. I am a very tenacious individual, and I have a relentless drive to overcome any obstacle that is put in front of me. Every single day is a fight, and I fight not because I want to fight, but rather because I'm capable of fighting. I find that it is my moral obligation to do so. Now of course there are times when I get tired, worn down, discouraged. I lose a hell of a lot of battles, but do you know what? That doesn't matter. What matters is that I always come back to win the wars.

It is my firm belief that the only true failure in life lies in not trying. As long as you always get back up after life knocks you down, as long as you keep taking those steps forward, however small they may be, you are bound to succeed. This is the epitome of perseverance.

Fear

We as humans fear many things: failure, change, death, to name just a few. Why do we fear? Firstly, it's an instinctual response to help us avoid danger. However, as humans evolved and became more civilized, the need for this innate reaction gradually diminished.

We also become afraid, or fearful, of that which is unknown to us. We are creatures of habit, and we like to know what to expect in our day to day lives. We can liken fear to that moment when our chair of expectation is pulled out from under us. That feeling of startling disorientation as we expect to be sitting in a chair but somehow are falling to the ground instead. Our heart sinks, we panic, and for a split second our minds enter a state of confusion, encapsulated by nothing other than that of which we do not know. We then hit the ground, and a steady wave of reassurance washes over us as we realize that everything is okay. No more are we victim to the unknown, for we now know that the chair was pulled out from under us, and we need to do little more than to pick ourselves up from the ground, pull the chair in, and have a seat.

This analogy should make it clear that fear and over-thinking are two sides of the same coin. When unexpected occasions arise, calm yourself. Have faith in your circumstance, whatever it may be, for you were put into it for a reason. I always say that fear is nothing more than opportunity disguised as risk. When fear strikes, take a risk and run towards it. You'll come to find that the veil of fear will slowly diminish, thus revealing the opportunity behind it.

Exercise

Over the years I have come to find that exercise is absolutely vital to the protection of my well being. I currently go to the gym 6 days a week in order to stay one step ahead of my demons. I push myself as physically hard as I can at the gym, for the pain that comes with working out is nothing compared to what I deal with in my mind on an almost daily basis. I exhaust my body when I work out due to the carry over effect it has on my brain. After a good work out, my brain is too tired to play its usual tricks on me. When at the gym, my mind is at peace, something I truly cherish and look forward to every day.

If I happen to miss a scheduled workout at the gym, my day is usually DOA. I become severely depressed, and I see the world in black and white, as opposed to the beautiful colors I see on days that I get a good workout. My anxiety is ramped up, I have less energy, my executive functioning diminishes and I find it extremely hard to be productive.

Many people don't realize that physical fitness is, from my view, more mental than it is physical. When I push my body past the point of exhaustion, just as I feel the burn in my muscles, I can feel the burn in my mind as well. I start to hear that voice inside of me telling me to give up, to quit, that this is too hard. But when I choose not to listen to that voice I gain power over it, and this immediately generalizes into my everyday life, and the obstacles that I face on a daily basis.

Regret

Regret is perhaps the only feeling that serves absolutely no purpose in our lives. When we live our lives with regret, we are choosing to focus on an action. However, behind every action is a principle. When we let regret seep into our state of mind, we lose clarity of the principle that was behind the action we regret, and when we lose sight of that principle, any lesson we can possibly learn from the situation slowly starts to drift away. Regret is a feeling about the past, it is a roadblock when it comes to learning our lessons and bettering ourselves. When we are given the opportunity to learn, what do we have to regret?

We all know that everybody makes mistakes and poor decisions, but do we blame the steep grade of the earth when it comes to summiting a vast mountain? We can surpass the setback of regret in a simple 3-step process:

1. Recognize the action that is responsible for your feeling of regret.

2. Identify the principle behind that action.

3. Acknowledge that although some actions can be regrettable, principles rarely are.

Principles are the foundation of your moral compass. Just because your moral compass may take you in the wrong direction at times doesn't mean the intent behind it was wrong.

Picture yourself walking in the middle of a dense forest. You know that the closest exit is to the north, so you pull out your compass to guide you there. However, you actually end up walking south, thus finding yourself deeper in the forest. Your compass' intent (and your intent) was to take you out of the forest by walking north. If we boil it down to metaphysics, the blame lands not on the compass pointing north, but on the action of physically taking the steps in the wrong direction. The intent was there, the action not so much.

Have faith in the fact that your intention was evident! Once we are able to dissect our mistakes, and what went wrong in the calculation of our intent, we begin to shift from regretting our slipups to learning from them. We now become more knowledgeable when it comes to taking the correct actions to fulfill our intent, which in turn is guided by our principles.

Regret will eat you alive, it will consume you. It will make you lose faith in yourself for something that happened in the past, therefore putting your future endeavors into a state of uncertainty and apprehension.

No regrets. Ever. You can feel guilt, remorse, shame, etc., all of which are valid emotions, with each one serving an acceptable and productive purpose. However, to regret something means to wish it never happened, and to reiterate the all-important point of this chapter, when we take the time and energy to regret something from the past, we lose sight of the future. We lose sight of what lessons we can learn that will ultimately help us become a better person in the future. As Les Brown once said, "It doesn't matter what happened yesterday. What matters is, what are you going to do about it?"

Why do we suffer?

Some say that suffering is a choice. I like to pose it in a different light: If we accept that we as humans are prone to suffering, in the end we will not suffer.

Personally, I suffer a great deal, and I am just now learning how to accept this. That being said, however, I love the ideology behind the pre-Socratic philosopher Heraclitus. Known as "The Weeping Philosopher" Heraclitus believed that everything comes into being after going through some sort of natural struggle.

Our struggles, suffering included, make us who we are. We can either drown in our sorrows, or we can use them as floatation devices to motivate us to become all-around better individuals. As the famous African proverb goes "A smooth sea never made a skilled sailor". Your struggles define you in the long run, so when you hit rough waters, hold on to them with all your might!

Resiliency

Resiliency

Resiliency is perhaps one of the greatest traits to have. Being resilient has nothing to do with how successful you are, how hard you work or how fast you go. Resiliency is all about taking baby steps and not stopping. As Confucius once said, "It doesn't matter how slowly you go, as long as you do not stop".

We can best compare resiliency to water. Water can be one of the most peaceful and calmest substances on earth, yet can also be the most powerful. Water always gets to where it is headed, and rarely does anything block it's path.

"In the world, there is nothing more submissive and weak than water. Yet for attacking that which is hard and strong, nothing can surpass it." - Lao Tzu, founder of Taoism

If we learn to not focus on the our long-term goals, and to instead focus on each step we take, resiliency can be our greatest power.

Philosophy

As mentioned earlier, the ancient Greek philosopher Heraclitus believed that everything comes into being through strife.

Heraclitus lived in the 6th century B.C. and was known as "The Weeping Philosopher" due to the difficult life he lived. Now, what Heraclitus meant by this was that everything in the universe is formed through intense conflict, whether it be tectonic plates colliding into each other to form our beautiful mountains or waves crashing into a hillside, creating jaw-dropping seaside views or saplings using all thier might to sprout up through the densest and most rigid earth. Nothing came to be without some sort of natural struggle.

Now think about this for a moment...if this can be said for nature and the universe, which we are a part of, then why would we not say the same thing about ourselves? That the struggles we encounter in life only aid in our evolution as individuals?

Another core belief of Heraclitus was that we ourselves and everything around us is always in a state of flux, or change. He once said, "No man ever steps in the same river twice, for it is not the same river and he is not the same man". We as humans tend to fear change, for we find comfort in our expectations and certainty of routine. As an individual on the spectrum, I fear change more than most. Something as simple as not having my regular 1 ½ cups of oatmeal for breakfast is terrifying! Lol! I have come to find, however, that the world is constantly evolving, constantly developing and growing, due to change. If we, as individuals, learn to embrace the fear of change around us and within us, we too can enjoy the benefits of constantly developing and growing into the best versions of ourselves.

Fear is uncomfortable, it's supposed to be. It's an innate and instinctual reaction to protect us from possible danger. But in today's world, a lot of our fears are societal fears. Fear of change! Fear of failing. Fear of commitment, of love. Fear of letting others down. The fear of being vulnerable.

I once wrote in an article that fear, first and foremost, is nothing more than opportunity disguised as risk. Learn to run towards, and not away, from your fears, for behind every single fear in your life is a wondrous reward that you will only attain if you push through what frightens you.

More wise words from Heraclitus would be that "There is nothing permanent, except change". In order to prosper and live up to our full potential, we don't have much choice than to embrace the certainty that there will always be change, and the uncertainty of what that change will be. I think we can all agree that nobody wants to remain stagnant as an individual. Well, an antonym for stagnation, is change. ;)

We as humans are natural adapters. When we continually subject ourselves to new environments, circumstances, experiences and stimuli, our brains literally form new synaptic connections. It's safe to say that embracing change is a great workout for the brain. It becomes stronger, more efficient and is better adept at handling stressful situations.

For me, personally, I have always felt such a deep sense of comfort when I read ancient philosophy. To realize that humans have been combating their emotions, while struggling to maintain a sense of well-being, for over 3,000 years helps me realize that I am, BY FAR, not alone when I struggle with the same issues that have burdened mankind since its inception.

Parenting

To any parents who may be reading this book, I cannot overstate how vital and significant you are to your child's success. I always say that the parent holds the key to unlocking their child's full potential.

So love your child unconditionally. Fight for them with all your might. Listen to them when they're down and out, and perhaps most importantly, never second guess or question your actions as a parent. You know what's best for your child, and always remember this: If you do something out of love, it is never wrong.

ON THE OUTSIDE LOOKING IN

Being our own worst critic

We can easily give others advice about a situation, but when that advice applies to us, we don't seem to listen to ourselves.

Listening to our own advice seldom works. However, by knowing what advice to give others in a similar circumstance to ours, we by default already know the solution to our problem, yet we still don't take it upon ourselves to accept this Perhaps that's because we are not fully aware of the answer residing with us.

I believe that deep down, we all know how to get through each situation life hands out to us. Whether the answer is buried in our conscious or subconscious mind is up for debate, but it's in there, trust me. I speculate that the reason behind why we can be so hard on ourselves is that a part of us knows that the solution to our problem is right under our nose, yet we fail to see it. This ultimately results at us becoming frustrated with ourselves.

RUSSELL LEHMANN

The Law of Attraction

If we truly want society to be more accepting and under-
standing of others, the ball is in our court. Initiate the
change you wish to see in this world, and others will soon
follow.

Every single one of us is capable of instilling values,
morals and beliefs into others. Even the simplest show of
support can begin to unlock the secrets to one's success,
whether it's giving a smile to somebody you pass in a hall-
way, verbal praise after a risk is taken (regardless if they
succeeded or not) or just a simple hug after a long day. It
all starts with us.

Some of you have probably heard of the "Law of At-
traction". This is ultimately what I am talking about. It is
scientifically proven that our thoughts and our intentions
behind our actions send out electrical pulses from our
brains that in turn attract more of the same from others.

As Plato once stated:
"Like attracts like".

ON THE OUTSIDE LOOKING IN

RUSSELL LEHMANN

.

POETRY

RUSSELL LEHMANN

2002

RUSSELL LEHMANN

Happy Again

On the boat of St. Anthony's

There was an eight-year-old boy

Whose hair was bright and shiny

Along with his toy

5 The boat was docked

Ready to go

The engine turned on

And the boat just glowed

Up and down, down and up

10 Bounced the boat in the water

The dad was driving very fast

And then he spotted an otter

The dad was smiling

But the boy was crying

15 For he didn't have a floating device

There was none to be found

On the very big boat

For all the dad knew

The boy couldn't float

20 The boy was still crying

The boat sped up

Still crying and crying

And the dad had had enough

The boat turned around

25 Heading right for the dock

Once again the boat sped up

And none of them talked

At the dock they all got out

The dad tied the boat

30 And the kid wandered about

They hooked the boat up to the car

The trip home wouldn't be far

When they got home

ON THE OUTSIDE LOOKING IN

Mom was waiting outside

35 They all gave her a hug

And they all went inside

The mom had on a grin

But the dad and boy didn't

But inside, the two were happy again

40 So there they were, all happy inside

But the best part of all

Is that there together with pride

RUSSELL LEHMANN

Two-Word Poem

Pro basketball,

My future,

Shooting 3's,

Major dunks,

Dribbling fast,

Blocking shots,

Coaching some,

Championship won.

Dial-A-Poem

8 I watch the ball fly through the air

3 Then look left

3 People watch

4 The buzzer sounds

6 The ball soars through the net

5 Then I gr]asp, I just shot.

0 ...

Behind Closed Eyes

One day in the hospital of St. Mary,

A woman was giving birth to three.

At half past ten the procedure was done,

But the babies for some reason, weighed a ton.

Two were girls and one a boy,

Every day they were given toy after toy.

However, they lost interest in them very quick,

And everyone started wondering if they were sick.

The doctor wanted to take some tests,

Because he thought it would be for the best.

But before the doctor had that chance,

One of the babies asked him for a dance.

And out of the corner of the doctor's eye,

He saw the other two babies eating some pie.

ON THE OUTSIDE LOOKING IN

The doctor could not believe what he was seeing,

To add to that he saw a plant turn into a human being.

All of the babies' hands turned into barbequed ribs,

While the head of the doctor turned into a crib.

The three babies saw this and jumped into his head,

Then all closed their eyes and went to bed.

Until a baby woke up to the moonbeam,

And said to himself, it was just a dream.

RUSSELL LEHMANN

Only at Night

When I'm in bed trying to fall asleep

I soon notice that I have cold feet

I then fix that problem and go back to bed

But soon notice I have an itch on my head

I then fix that problem and try to fall asleep

I then hear my sister's music going bo, bop, be, beep

I then fix that problem and go back to bed

I then hear throbbing on my arm

But it's not, it's the alarm

ON THE OUTSIDE LOOKING IN

RUSSELL LEHMANN

2009

RUSSELL LEHMANN

Your Poem

You asked me to write a poem for you

Which I agreed to do

I'll just keep it short and simple

This is what I think of you

You seem like a wonderful person

Who knows how to listen

Who is also understanding

And never asks the wrong questions

I still have a lot to learn about you

Which I am excited to do

You still have a lot to learn about me

And I hope you're excited, too

RUSSELL LEHMANN

You asked me to write a poem for you

Which I agreed to do

I'll just keep it short and simple

This is what I think of you

You Haven't Fought My Fight

Crack YOU SAY IT WILL BE OKAY

YOU HAVEN'T FAUGHT MY FIGHT, SO HOW COULD YOU KNOW?

YOU THINK YOU KNOW THE WAY THAT I THINK

YOUR ARROGANCE IS A DISTURBANCE

DON'T MIND ME NOW

FOR YOU HAVE BETTER THINGS TO DO

FEEL FREE TO TREAT ME LIKE A ROCK

THAT IS IN the path in front of you

I KNOW WHO I AM, AND I KNOW WHAT I WANT

I BELIEVEd you were my guide

To take me down that better path

I forgot I was that rock that you kicked aside

You made me jump over so many HURDLES

Higher and higher they became

I fell on my face, ten-fold; defaced

But I'm as tough as a rock; I won't degrade

You took my life for granted

You destroyed my self-esteem

But in the end that only made me stronger

I'm the rolling rock that grows no green

I BLEED MY FEAR; you cauterize yours

You keep it all inside

Afraid to leave your precious glass house

I'm that rock that you threw with pride

I MAY NOT SPEAK A LOT, YOU SPEAK A LITTLE MORE

MY WORDS SHOW MY VALUES, YOUR WORDS

ON THE OUTSIDE LOOKING IN

SHOW YOUR MASK

MY VALUES SHOW MY GOALS, YOUR MASK HAS NOTHING TO SHOW

YOUR DEMEANOR IS PITIFUL, YOUR FACE IS ICE COLD

I THINK WHAT I FEEL

YOU THINK WHAT YOU WANT/NEED

YOU ARE REPULSIVELY SELFFISH

YOU ARE ONE SICKENING SLEEZE

YOU HAVE A MISERABLE LIFE, ONE YOU DENY

YOU FEEL NOT FOR OTHERS, JUST FOR YOUR-SELF

YOU COMPARE YOURSELF TO PEOPLE LOWER THAN YOU

THIS MAKES YOU CONTENT, FOR HOW COULD YOU LOSE?

YOU HAVE PUT ME DOWN

BUT NOW I'M ON TOP

YOU ARE NOT WORTH ANYTHING, NOT EVEN
REVENGE

YOUR MIND, YOUR SOUL, YOUR HEART ARE
ALL WORTHLESS

YOU WASTE SPACE ON THIS PLANET

AS WELL AS WHAT WE BREATHE

ONE LAST THING I SHOULD /WILL SAY IS

YOU'RE AN IGNORAMUS TO ME

The Key to My Heart

It's the key to my heart, the depiction that is missing

Determined when I read into it, but then the book goes missing

The night time is the best time, without a doubt it's true

I look forward to the morning but dread the afternoon

It's at night that I'm alive; my need is to take action

This need is blocked by me; I do not take advantage of this passion

Bottom line, every day, declines me of my mind

I might as well be sleeping, which is my better time

RUSSELL LEHMANN

The Hurricane

As I look through the window of the tower lit high

The spread of the ocean forever moves

Everywhere, the rocks protrude

The mystic sky, dark with fury

Reflects its visage against the waves

The sight of an augury

The atmosphere around, so sordid indeed

The rage is so pertinent

Cloud nine is absent

The wickedness of its eye

It shall be malignant

ON THE OUTSIDE LOOKING IN

The horror it shall imply

I stand witness to this view

My eyes soon succumb

My thoughts become numb

The curse draws closer

How dismal and odious

For there is no answer

The sea grows dark

The tower's light is no more

The demon has come ashore

The victims so negligible

For their unknown fate

Will never be livable

The doom has arrived

RUSSELL LEHMANN

There is no transition

As all collide

Everything so decrepit

All is to rot

The horror has been brought

The Day is Over

The day is over, yet today has just begun

My mind is killing me, what do I do? My life is done

Make it literal! Go to the closet, pick up your gun

It's loaded, cocked, and ready to have some fun

What the hell am I doing here, living a life like this?

Is your life a lie? Why the hell do you exist?

I have no love in my life, not even one damn kiss

That's why you have a gun; don't go cut your god-damned wrists!

All of this is getting to me, all that is inside

That's why you have me here, so I can tell you when to die

Now go and get your gun, pull the trigger, give it
a try

If you do it properly, this will be our last goodbye

I'll walk over to the closet and pick up the gun for
you

That's a good-boy; grip it tight, you know what to
do

All I want is a better life! Will this make my dream
come true?

All you need to know, is that this is long overdue

Positive Opponents

The devil is strange

How strange would I say?

Strange enough to punish fiends

When we think he's depraved

Villains are good

How good would I say?

Good enough to teach us sense

When their faults are displayed

Words are too simple

How simple would I say?

Simple enough

But yet too complex to explain

Virtues are dire

How dire would I say?

Dire enough to let loose egos

And make one's character dissipate

Thoughts are obscure

How obscure would I say?

Obscure enough to deal out conflict

When there is no need to debate

Nothing

There is nothing, nothing, my thoughts are just nothing

How could I be here, if everything is nothing?

For I do not know what was, I know not what will be

My eyes look around, but there is nothing to see

I stand here alone, but how do I know

If everything is nothing, how could I know?

Why keep myself company, when there is nothing to be?

I stand here alone, for I am nothing to me

I know not what is nothing, it means nothing to me

But how do I know it means nothing to me?

RUSSELL LEHMANN

All these thoughts merely mean not a thing

If everything is nothing, then what could nothing mean?

Nothing knows me, it knows me well

How could it be that it knows me so well?

I have nothing to fear, for I now know what it means

The real meaning of nothing, is the real meaning of me

My Dream

My dream is just that

It's a dream they all say

A life so luxurious

A dream so cliché

"Be realistic!" they proclaim

It's a statement of control

I disregard their ignorance

As I know what my hard work is for

They criticize me,

"That will not be your life!"

This just adds fuel

To my fire that is rife

Why should I give up?

What point would that have?

It would make my life worthless,

No purpose to be had

They should know better,

Than to underestimate me

My drive will never stop

My drive they'll never beat

I'm a Fool for You

I've already fallen for you, but I don't even know you

We haven't even met, but somehow I adore you

I can't get you out of my head; thoughts of you are stuck like glue

The pain is starting to progress; I am depressed without you

We're supposed to meet each other, but something's telling me we won't

I've got to get this mess together; I'm going insane being alone

I'm waiting in the rain for you; I guess that I'll go home

The flowers drop to the ground, as I trace back this lonely road

I need to be with you, I'll wait for you, just to be cruel

A broken heart will be my death; I'll put away the

rope and stool

I'll throw my whole life away, if it means that we'll be two

I'm a fool, but I don't care, this is all that I can do

Hail to the Earth!

Hail to the Earth, for she may never perish!

Hail to the Earth, for all life she will reminisce!

Hail to the Earth, for all the minds she has brought forth!

Hail to the Earth, for to all life she gave birth!

Hail to the pastures, all plastered with green!

Hail to the seas, for they are the kings!

Hail to the gods, who protect all of our sights!

Hail to the Earth, for she is our light!

Hail to the doves, whose peace we adore!

Hail to the trees, whose love is evermore!

Hail to the valleys, who offer a choice!

Hail to the Earth, for she is our voice!

RUSSELL LEHMANN

Hail to the mountains, who proffer hope when one's in doubt!

Hail to the clouds, which prevail through our droughts!

Hail to the streams, for they restore our hearts!

Hail to the Earth, for she was our start!

Hail to the life, which encircles our minds!

Hail to the times, for our paths they define!

Hail to the words, which advance our race!

Hail to the Earth, for she is our saving grace!

Hail to the feelings, which direct our scruples!

Hail to the friendship, which fills all of our holes!

Hail to the failures, for they guide our directions!

Hail to the Earth, for she is our protection!

Hail to the love, for without our souls would fade!

Hail to the misery, for its absence shall void pray!

ON THE OUTSIDE LOOKING IN

Hail to the hate, for there would be no good!

Hail to the Earth, for all she has withstood!

Hail to the Earth, for she may never perish!

Hail to the Earth, for all life she will reminisce!

Hail to the Earth, for all the minds she has brought forth!

Hail to the Earth, for to all life she gave birth!

Egos Will Kill

The congregates all stared at him

What a despicable looking man!

With a face of white and an eerie grin

No being would be his friend

Each pair of eyes would stalk him

What a lift of self-esteem!

No more their lives, depressing and grim

For they have been redeemed!

A wicked sight this surely was

An oral slaying of one's heart

His soul will soon rise, and at their cost

Their lives will fall apart

Dark Side of Me

This is the dark side of me that no one has ever seen before

I've let it out, from my heart, and now it is no more ignored

Released into the state of me that I've never before explored

I've turned my back on my soul, the very thing that I've adored

Since I was young, to which I clung, when my back was against the door

And I now have myself asking, a question that I've never asked before

Who am I, where am I, is my old life now no more?

I've taken the wrong exit before, and until yester-day I still had sworn

To the lord, that I will fight with all my might just to save my rapport

With myself, when things get rough, but that part
of me is no more

I've shed my skin, it's in the trash, it's in the past,
this time surpassed

By greater good, or so I'm told; this dark side of me
will outlast

Any gracious thoughts of mine, most of which
have already passed

From my mind, to the dirt, six feet under the wilt-
ing grass

If I do not know you, then why should I care about
you?

Don't come to me; don't talk to me, for I will look
right through you

My respect for others is no more, please don't get
this wrong, for this is true

The dark side of me has come out, and there is
nothing you can do

Carve my Heart

My mind, my soul

Don't take it away

If you lose my faith today

My respect for you will stray

The crash of these waves

Will soon spray the array

Of the spite you displayed

When you paved the way

For all hell to break loose

I can still feel the blaze

Of the fire that you made

From the hatred that you gave

Your actions have played

That same somber song of faith

With the break in the middle

Of the "F" and the "H"

So bring with you your blade

For I'll give way to the pain

I'll give way to your ways

Of the vindictiveness you crave

So here I am, take what you may;

Carve my heart out today

A Day in Darfur

His name was Jabari, from the city of the slain

There was no one in sight, as his body lay maimed

For hours and hours, at this spot he laid

His feelings were numb, as he continued to pray

His world was now empty, with nothing in sight

His body left behind, as his soul saw the light

His brothers, his sisters

They all face these crimes

His brothers, his sisters

They know nothing of these crimes

The yard will be full, it has been full

The red crosses have been struck

Their bodies are salvaged by silk and needle

The rest is up to luck

For years it has ensued, and for years it will not pass

The flames that one encounters, is nothing new, alas

All rule appears inept, the dwellers weak and frail

No hope for help to come, for the anguish will prevail

ON THE OUTSIDE LOOKING IN

RUSSELL LEHMANN

2010

RUSSELL LEHMANN

Wars Will Never End

The wars have started long ago

For wars will never end

The women and children, all in woe

As their souls gradually ascend

The deep depression, that strikes one's mind

Dreadfully stays its course

For in time, one's thoughts grow blind

And soon show signs of no remorse

The darkness that prevails the light

Is guided by its master

The orders given are in spite

For ignorance leads to disaster

RUSSELL LEHMANN

The bliss was taken, long ago

The misery will never end

The women and children will someday know

That their souls have reached their end

Troubled Young Kid

"People like you don't deserve to live!"

These were the thoughts of a troubled young kid

The quote likely aimed at people he feared

His thoughts were as real, as his intentions were clear

RUSSELL LEHMANN

The Wild Hunt

Close your eyes, my boy, for the hounds have ar-
rived

Descending from the sky

Gwynn app Nudd, King of Annwn[4]

Leads them on with his dreadful cry

Dare not, my boy, sleep today

Keep your spirit tightly bound

For if you partake in your dreams

In their parade you will be found

Thou shall not, my boy, take interest

In this hunt for the Moss Maiden[5]

Lest you be snatched by wicked hands

Who'll bring you to their deathly haven

ON THE OUTSIDE LOOKING IN

Fear not, my boy, for we have no control

Of the outcome that has been destined

There is blood to be spilt, or a plague to be spread

Ensuing the sure death of kith and kin

We are, my boy, fated to be prey

Of this wild hunt before us

So take part with me to relish this sight

Before we hear the devil's chorus

4In Welsh mythology, Gwynn app Nudd was the leader of the underworld, known as Annwn.

5In German folklore, the Moss people were fairies who were "grey and old-looking, hairy, and clad in moss." (Thiselton-Dyer, 1889)

The Mormon

I was something, until I met you

Now I'm something more, this could not be more true

I was on my way up, when I first saw you

Who would have thought, that all the courage that grew

All the strength that has brewed

Was all because of you

You thought you could dismantle me; don't stray from what is true

Taking your shirt off in front of teenage girls was pretty lewd

Who'd want to show off by flopping their belly like a balloon?

You supposedly a Mormon, of which I could make
a crack or two

Maybe you drink your little tipples, and hoped that
no one knew

But I'm not low like you, that's how I am and how
I do

We sit face-to-face, you seem confused, you don't
move

You knew you were the issue, but you did not
know what to do

That doesn't surprise me at all, please tell me
something new

Suddenly you're alerted, someone's yelling at you

You flew out of your chair, and out the door you
blew

What happened to being macho? I thought that's
what you do

You treated me like garbage: "Oh, did I forget to
tell you?

RUSSELL LEHMANN

You came here for nothing. I thought you already knew."

It took me an hour and half to get here, what the hell is wrong with you?

This happened more than three times, just the way you wanted, too

You can't even imagine what I wanted to do to you

Be glad I'm not a psycho; be glad you still can move

I was just a kid, so for you I've got some news

If you do that to another kid, I will come and find you

Maybe you would receive a bruise, maybe it would be your life you lose

I cannot think for you, but here is what I suggest you do

Go crawl into a hole and try to find the soul in you

If it can't be done, I think pity would be due

ON THE OUTSIDE LOOKING IN

Even though you're out of my life, I still think of you

You probably forgot all about me, which is probably good news

Because if you saw me now, you'd know what you contributed to

Your prejudice made me stronger, your ignorance made me new

Your arrogance gave me a life that is too good to be true

And even though you're still wasted space, my thanks go out to you

RUSSELL LEHMANN

The Healthy Mind of a Cannibal

I'm driving down the street

Looking for someone to meet

Maybe I'll kidnap them, torture them

And then eat them as meat

I know people think my mind is sick

I think my mind is perfectly fine

Why is it abnormal to eat human flesh,

And to drink blood when I dine?

Anyways, back to my job

I need someone to find

My stomach is rumbling now

It's past my dinner time

ON THE OUTSIDE LOOKING IN

Oh! At last! I found someone

To capture and confine!

I'll put a bag over his head

And throw him in my van to make him mine

I finally get home

I am ecstatic as can be!

I'll go pull out my butcher knife

This should do the job for me

I walk my dinner to the basement

And push him down the stairs

I follow right behind

Let's see how this will fare

I pull the bag off of his head

So he can see the gruesome act

Of how my feast will be prepared

RUSSELL LEHMANN

Should I slice or should I hack?

I proceed to lay him on the ground
So eager to attack
He struggled a bit, but now he is bound
As I begin my gruesome act

I slowly stroke his toenails
As I pick up my butcher knife
I pluck each and every piggy hat off
Oh the rush of controlling one's life!

I proceed to do the same to his hands
And eventually pull out his teeth
I feel a joyous song coming on!
Please dinner, sing with me!

I work my way up to his eyes

ON THE OUTSIDE LOOKING IN

Of which I carve out with my knife

I will save them for my appetizer

Oh my! What a delight!

I work my way back down to his feet

Of which I break with all my might

I twist them round and round and round

As he screams with such delight!

Now it's time to get down to business

I chop off his arms and legs!

His pleas are so amusing

It's so exciting when he begs!

But no longer will he beg

For I am going for his head

I slice right through his skin

And put his soul to bed

There is now just a torso on the ground,

His head and limbs are no more

I threw that junk into the garbage,

For the best part is the core!

My oven has been pre-heated

But this plan I must withdraw

For I am so hungry, and he looks so tasty

I cannot resist eating him raw!

His flesh is so delicious!

His organs oh so tender

His veins so plump and juicy

This feast I shall always remember!

For dessert I think I'll eat his heart

For dipping sauce I shall use is blood

Oh my! The blood! So thick and rich!

ON THE OUTSIDE LOOKING IN

The taste is such a rush!

This banquet has been so bountiful

Oh, what a perfect day this was!

How fun it is to take and kill

A man who deserves my love!

Sometime soon I should repeat this

For how I love to eat such treats

Maybe I'll go out tomorrow

To shop for more to eat

I'm driving down the street

Looking for someone to meet

Maybe I'll kidnap them, torture them

And then eat them as meat

RUSSELL LEHMANN

The Conscience of Man

Little do know

That inside of us grows

Miniature men

Who fight for our souls

Some good, some bad

Some sad, some glad

To most seem transparent

When one's out to gad

They look after our species

Though they rarely agree

On the decisions we make

For our blind eyes they foresee

ON THE OUTSIDE LOOKING IN

The trouble we make

In the events we partake

Are none for their pleasure

They recognize our mistake

But who shall guide them?

In their troubles that stem

 From the ignorant thoughts

Of their shell that is man

For they venture alone

In the dark they condone

They shall fight no more

Their weakness has shown

Free from their shell

They no longer dwell

In their shell's hollow heart

For their ship has set sail

A soul, unprotected

A soul, now infected

With nerves of pure ice

Is a soul, now neglected

The love is no more

The heart is ignored

The mind is a follower

To its master no more

So soon said and done

The evil has won

For in hell awaits

The end of their run

My Whole Life Has Been a Mess

I wasn't blessed, f*** that

My whole life has been a mess

I haven't been normal, I'm a freak you could call me

But I'll f***ing stomp you, I don't have any sympathy

I lost my only friend, when the time was supposed to be merry

I wanted to f***ing die, I had had enough of this misery

You could say I've made progress, throughout my whole life

But I don't give a F***, I want a family and a wife

Sure, I might be young, but that's the feeling I have

Just thinking these thoughts shows me the life I could've had

People discriminate me, like I need that, too

If I could, I'd walk up to that Mormon and blast him in two

People ask me why I don't talk, I say nothing back

You can go f*** yourselves, you stupid a**holes

The only contact I had, was with my very best friend

He was my life, I still cry whenever I think of him

That's F***ED up, why the f*** did he have to go?

I f***ing HATE my life, now that I am alone

He was my little baby; I'd protect him with my life

I swear if someone ever hurt him, I'd take their F***ING life!

I am so lonely, I want someone with whom my love I could share

My life is so f***ing boring, and God doesn't seem to care

ON THE OUTSIDE LOOKING IN

I don't want to be a teen, and party and s***

I would rather be married and run away from this s***

But that's not gonna happen, the past ten years I have tried

I am running out of energy, I am so sick of my life

That's it; my whole life is f***ed up

I need someone to help me

Please

My Best Friend

"There is no greater sorrow than to recall happiness in times of misery." ~ Danté Alighieri

I'm back after six months

That stone had gotten to me more than once

But now it's gone

Two days back was the whisper of "so long"

It was supposed to be temporary

But it's almost been two years

I dared not to go near it, just because of the fear

I was sick of wiping my face with my shirt to get the tears

But as I write this, the tears start to appear

The pain hurts so much, and it will never go away

It's here to stay, but that's okay because it is the

only way

To remember the life that we had together, and to this day

I beat myself with every single hit that I can take

I lashed out at you when all you wanted was to play

It was your way of telling me that you only had a few days

Because after that all you did was try to get away

You hid from me, but I brushed it off; a mistake that turned so grave

I was so stupid to take for granted the life you gave to me

And when I finally asked you what was wrong, it was just too late

This wasn't fate, it was God's way to turn my life into misery

I love you so much I cannot even begin to say

All of the things that I would do to spend time with you today

RUSSELL LEHMANN

You were my best friend, but like I said God took
that away

I try not to think of you; No, I love you too much

When I do my heart gets crushed, the pain, it's just
too much

I guess it's self-centered, it's my emotional crutch

But this is what I signed up for, the second that we
touched

I'll never forget you Gilbert, you turned me into a
man

I was and always will be your biggest fan

People don't understand how you could be my
best friend

My only friend, and in the end, I wished it was
pretend

I'll never forget you Gilbert, you are in my heart
until the end

And the end will just begin, when I see you once
again

Mr. Halley[6]

Year 1692 is when that blasphemous buffoon

Revealed the dwellings of man's mind

A song of sorrow tune

In hollow earth his thoughts aren't welcome

I put forth fire on my everlasting

Souls that were in tombs

He shall not last in man's own head

For their psyches reside with me

And slumber in my bed

My home, he thought, is bright as day

He knew not it is the flames

RUSSELL LEHMANN

Feeding on likes of him for play

The expanding air of my own singed lives

Releases to the world above

Making for the glacial lights

Dare not his ideas flow

Through the river of the blood

Ensuing to the float to those unbeknownst

Down! Down! I'll come to pluck him from the sky

21 grams smothered in a fire

So hot the blaze will cry

Soon, not enough, he will accompany me

Into my dear bed

Filled with minds – temper free

Hesitance not taken to his own wit's dying out

ON THE OUTSIDE LOOKING IN

It is his time for him to be tucked in

No more spews from his shriveled spout

Invincible in future times of the past and present

I shall remain the captor of all thoughts

Mr. Halley, you will learn your lesson

6Edmond Halley was an English astronomer, geophysicist, mathematician, and meteorologist recognized for computing the orbit of Halley's Comet, which later took his name. In 1692, Halley proposed a theory that the Earth was hollow.

Psychadelic Poem

Part I

His belly flippity-flopped, his peers were so funny

He looked like a bunny when he hoppity-hop hopped

From flopping to hopping, to skipping and stop-ping

He entered his house, his sister was so funny

Up to his bedroom, he jumpitty-jump jumped

He opened his window and looked down at the water

He jumped right out and flippity-flop flopped

His belly now red from flippity-flop flopping

He climbed out of the water, and he shookitty-shook shook

The water from his hair

ON THE OUTSIDE LOOKING IN

Part II

Into the forest she goes, wandering around

She looks down at the little buggies on the ground

Each with four different hands

Waving to her in grand fashion

Each little buggy began to sprout legs

Not buggy legs, no,

But human legs, yes

Crooked and thin, those human legs were

At the end were ten toes

Not on both legs but each

One little buggy walks toward her

And reaches out his hand

To offer a handshake

She shakes the buggy's hand

But let go he will not

The other buggies jump on her

They laugh when she screams

RUSSELL LEHMANN

Part III

A man was walking in the Dusky Wood

When he spotted an evil shade

No, it was a monkey, a monkey in a tree!

Yes! A monkey! And the monkey had wings!

The man hit the ground, laughing as hard as can be

The monkey then flew off, flapping its wings

The man stopped laughing, for now he was angry

His fury consumed him as he chased after the monkey

He came upon the monkey, who was sitting on the ground

The man started laughing as hard as can be

The monkey then flew off, high above the trees

The man became angry, screaming at the top of his lungs

He continued through the Dusky Wood

Until he stumbled onto some bricks

Yellow were the bricks

ON THE OUTSIDE LOOKING IN

Yes, yellow! Yes, Yellow!

The man ran in circles, laughing hard as can be

He followed the brick road which was so very long

 When he reached the end of the road

There was nothing in sight

Except for some squares

Some black and some white

The road had taken him to an eerie chess board

The man became angry, angry as can be

He stepped onto the board, where a queen he did see

The queen approached him, so short was she

She asked the man what he wanted to be

"A knight? A rook? Maybe even my king?

No, I think not, for a pawn you shall be!"

The man started laughing as hard as can be

Not fond of this, the queen stated a decree

"A decree?" thought he, "For what could it be?"

RUSSELL LEHMANN

Part IV

There was a man and a bike path, nothing else

The man was picked up and dropped onto the bike path

The bike path gladly let the man walk all over its brand new tar

"What a generous bike path!" the man thought to himself

He continued to walk all over the path

When he came upon a rotten peach

From where this peach came, he did not know

He asked the bike path, but it too did not know

The man began to stare at the peach

For six hours he had stared,

When the bike path finally joined in

"How surreal!" exclaimed the man,

Still staring at the peach

"How did this peach get here,

If there is no peach tree?"

The bike path answered

ON THE OUTSIDE LOOKING IN

This most difficult question

"Some things cannot be explained"

Kent State

A gruesome day in 1970, blood was splattered about

The bodies of innocent ones were lying face down

A young man was shot once, collapsing to the ground

In memoriam Jeffery, your spirit abounds

Just 19 years old, constructing a quote of pure peace

Allison stared death straight in the eyes

Not at all afraid of what she was to meet

Her essence conquered her demise

Paranoia unfortunately, set its eyes upon Bill

An innocent passerby of pure hell

ON THE OUTSIDE LOOKING IN

A man so young, his whole life he had to fulfill

Not again would he hear the toll of the bell

A walk across the green, turned into a resting in the red

For young Sandra, a woman of smarts and compassion

For a bullet was approaching her, aimed just below her head

A death brought about in such a ruthless fashion

Thirteen innocent victims, four of whom perished

Were tossed into a world of such mayhem

All lives of such value, always to be cherished

May such a calamity never happen again

RUSSELL LEHMANN

Iraq Invades

Little Jimmy looks out of the front door

At what seems to be a beautiful day

This is untrue for Jimmy, though

For those thoughts have gone away

His heart is racing;

Sweat is dripping from his brow

He takes a deep breath, and takes a step

He is so frightened to go out

He can't take any more of these sights

Blood over here, blood over there

Bodies maimed right in front of his eyes

It's no wonder he's so scared

ON THE OUTSIDE LOOKING IN

His best friend was killed, when he stepped on a mine

His big brother, sent to God's lair

How foolish he was, for he got in the line

Of fire, bullets spewing everywhere

Jimmy is oh so angry

Angry of the Red, White and Black

Which in the center, states "God is great"

But to Jimmy, God has turned his back

On the fighting that is going on

Between his human beings

Killing each other with guns and bombs

Or at least, that is how it seems

The smell of death is haunting,

As is the stench of burning skin

Everyday seems never ending

This world is far too sick for him

He has seen bodies melt,

All turning to slush

Lonely limbs on the ground,

And faces that have been crushed

Jimmy used to love his life; his world had seemed so grand

Until his country was attacked, or as they say "protect"

This war was for the greater good, man vs. man

Some geniuses they had to be, it had the opposite effect

His neighborhood is no more,

All the houses are torn apart

Everyone trying to escape the horror

As the Red, White and Black begin to march

Jimmy cannot take this anymore,

ON THE OUTSIDE LOOKING IN

All the death and gore that he sees
Mangled bodies, tied in hordes
He wants to be set free

He finally takes that second step,
For he's not scared anymore
All of the fight that he once had, left
He now knows what to do, unlike before

He walks down the street toward the base
The base of the Red, White and Black
And proceeds to stare the men in the face
As he reaches behind his back

This war will never be understood
In survivor's broken minds
This war will never stand for good
It has broken the red line

I'm Happy

Don't think I'm not a happy person

Don't think I don't know how to have fun

Maybe it's just that I want to blend in

Maybe I just want to be you for once

You start to talk to me and act real happy

I get sick of that, so I ignore you

You might think I'm rude, you might think I'm mean

Well you've got it wrong, I'm just jealous of you

You don't know me; you think my life is just like
yours

Oh, I'm sorry, you don't have any friends?

When you talk your mind gets taken over by nerves?

I don't think so, so put those thoughts to an end

ON THE OUTSIDE LOOKING IN

You're lucky your mind isn't messed up

You're lucky that you have an active life

Why is it my life that had to be snubbed?

Rejected by you with no contrite

RUSSELL LEHMANN

God Made Me Who I Am

God made me who I am today

God took me to where I am today

He helped me behave in a way

That was impossibly fitting

To be locked into my soul

And be progressive without

My brain is shouting at me

Because I won't let it out

I can't help but keep it confined

Inside of my mind that once died

At the age of 12 but has since been revived

I probably won't let it out

In fear of being a freak

ON THE OUTSIDE LOOKING IN

Rain gut of the top of the, gut of the rain for the top of the

That's my head's motto every time that I speak

To that guy in the gym who I never wanted to meet

Or any other person that I come across in the streets

So leave it to me

To be all that I can be

Even if that means I freeze

When you try to warm up to me

Get Well

You have no friends

You have that special wish that you commend

You finally met the person of your dreams

But f*** the feeling it's pretend

You were so excited; you were climbing the ladder of love

But then you fell down the rungs; you're starting to think that there's no one above

That watches over you; instead he watches you!

He torments you! Like a f***ing flat tire your heart blew

You wish you could go back, back to when you were ten

You were so popular; Yes, sir, you were the man

But that f***in' metal in your mouth didn't give a damn

Blow your f***ing brains out! In this life a chance you didn't stand

But this is now; there's no denying the last ten years have been pure hell

Robbed of a childhood, your heart pounded while your brain swelled

Your old friends walked the bridge over the pit where you just fell

But now I guess the time has come, to stop dwelling and get well

RUSSELL LEHMANN

Discrimination Kills

A black man was walking down the street, going home

A car drove by, shot him point blank, now he's gone

He left behind a family; wife, daughter and son

A gay man was walking down the street, all covered in blood

Three bullets in his head, and two punctured lungs

In five steps he collapsed, the victim of three men having some fun

A Jewish man was walking down the street, happy as can be

Three minutes later, he was cornered into a back alley

He was jumped, mugged and thrown into the street

ON THE OUTSIDE LOOKING IN

A white man was walking down the street

Eager to get home to his beautiful family

This feat he did complete, for he was left in peace

RUSSELL LEHMANN

Cursed to be Normal

I was cursed to be normal, the normality of strange

God must have been drunk when He put together
my brain

I feel like I've been stuck at level 1 of this game

This game of tolerating pain, which I have done
without gain

Problems with me are too much to feel ashamed

Of what has been going on inside of my brain

Since day 1 x 30 days multiplied by 72 ways

I have proclaimed I need help, to change my way
of self-esteem

For it has been high everyday

Even though it seems there are no means,

To confiscate the compliments I put away in my
dreams

ON THE OUTSIDE LOOKING IN

This part of me seems so ugly in the way

That it seems to deem my inner retard everyday

I'm sorry if that offends you in some close-minded way

But just think, this thing inside of me comes out everyday

Much to my dismay

I feel like I should fly away up to the heavens

And ask God

Why me?

I was 12 when I said I was 13

I wanted to fit in and not lose myself,

Over this OCD

So I sat in C-3, for five straight, strenuous weeks

Until the doctor came and told me

That my treatment was complete

I was free

I was happy at first but later on that day

I grew angry because the doctor didn't tell me

That there was another school I had to see

Simple minds and simple times occurred inside that school

Except for me, for I had my hood up

And drifted off to some tunes

When I was forced into a room of complete solitude

All while knowing that those people, had played me for a fool

All they ever did, was look for somebody to screw

Mrs. Yappity-Yap and Mr. Do-This-And-Do-That

Were so irritating! They thought they had me in their laps

But I just blew them off and took three-hour naps

Until my mom picked me up, and drove me away from that trap

I would look back and pray that I wouldn't have to go back

ON THE OUTSIDE LOOKING IN

These ideas stem from a mind

That has been through too much in its time

So calloused it has become, in its long worn out life

From attempts to colonize the insults it has survived

And throw them off to the side

I wish I could give them my life, and see the fear in their eyes

As they cry and apologize for the damage they have done

To a life, so young

And now that life is saying "So long,

You are in the past

For my life has just begun."

Since day one I've been in crisis mode

I cannot even begin to relate

To what a normal life feels like

Until I look it in the face

But still then

I don't see any eyes, ears, nose or mouth

I just see a black hole

That is the epitome

Of what my life is about

But I just keep on staring in the mirror

Trying to figure my life out

My OCD is bittersweet

In the fact that it hurts me and my family

In the fact that it forces me, to always perform superbly

In the fact that when I go to sleep, I count sheep infinitely

In the fact that I cannot stop, until I succeed in everything

Until I'm close to fainting

I train hard because training

Puts a positive reinforcement in me

That I can be anything that I want to be

ON THE OUTSIDE LOOKING IN

Say hello to this positive reinforcement, please

His name is OCD

And right now, he is the manipulator that I want him to be

But then there's a flip side, for he can always turn real mean

He becomes so very angry, that he thinks the thoughts in me

And spits out the nasty spews, of his tongue indefinitely

And unfortunately, his tongue is the one I use to speak

So please, somebody help me

For this OCD

Has become the being of existence

That is supposed to be me

A Soon to be Victim

A soon to be victim has come into my sights

A gun in my left hand, a knife in my right

This man in front of me destroyed my whole life

The last breath he will draw, will be drawn tonight

He acted like my friend, but he doesn't know me

He acted like I'm slow, but that's contradictory

I just tuned him out, for there was no point of listening

He kept moving his lips, but I don't hear what I see

Let's not get into details; it would take me my whole day

I'll just say his act elevated in each and every way

He filled me with rage, much to my dismay

And that's why I have chosen to end his life today

ON THE OUTSIDE LOOKING IN

RUSSELL LEHMANN

2011

RUSSELL LEHMANN

Murderer

Monday was the day, that you paralyzed me with pain

Destroying my whole world, with the most un-bearable strain

Of depression that I maintained, for weeks without any gains

All while leaving a stain, on my heart that you ripped and maimed

That day was the closest, that I had ever maintained

The thought of having my brains rain

Upon my lifeless body, from a colt .45 aimed

At the origin of all things gained, at the origin of all my pain

You tore me up, but now I'm coming back stronger

RUSSELL LEHMANN

Yes, I'm still depressed, but yet I am no longer

Unsure of my will to live on, an idea so heavily pondered

Those thoughts are collected, and are now much calmer

I sang a song so somber

But the harp's strings are being pulled no longer

What you did was neither right, or wrong or,

Right; you killed the feelings I had forever longed for

They say that everything, happens for a reason

Hinting that everything, will soon work itself out

But what if that everything, goes back on its promise?

Like my everything did; burying my heart six feet down

I dream of seeing you again, but I know that dream will not come true

ON THE OUTSIDE LOOKING IN

I'm moving on without you, for I now know I'm too good for you

You made me want to kill, from all the sadness that you brewed

But the only thing I will kill, are the memories of being with you

Nobody

Nobody understands the pain that I feel

Nobody knows that I can't live with these ills

Nobody can fathom my mental scars that won't heal

Nobody realizes that their problems are nil

My biggest fear is people, but let's not forget food

I'm plagued by agoraphobia and anorexia, too

I hate the outside world and mirrors kill my mood

I can't help but think, why can't I be like you?

If I were weak, I'd end it now just to escape all the pain

But I love my family too much, and I know my strength will be regained

ON THE OUTSIDE LOOKING IN

Even though I'll never attain, an ounce of victory in this game

I'll still strive for the impossible, even if there is nothing to gain

Life: It's a Game

Every day, I'd wake up to play the same damn game

I'd take my dose of pride to face the boss of this domain

Wash it down with fear; I took some strides but made no gains

All the kids ever tried to do was f— with my brain

I kept to myself; I never bothered anyone

Maybe unintentionally because of how pathetic I'd become

I was so scatterbrained; I let down my family as a son

I was so worthless, not even fit to be the victim of a gun

I would stare at the wall, zoned out, deep thoughts accompanying music

You told me I was accomplishing s—. Madam, screw it

Your behavior was so transparent; don't even try to make excuses

Your job was your life; I was your pawn and you damn well knew it

Internal Warrior

An internal warrior

Lights the fire of fate, the fire of hate

To escape the stakes of a great

Who suffocates the oxygen

That flows through the gates

To the fire of fate, to the fire of hate

An internal warrior

Speaks not of his foes

For they succumb to the blows

From the power of his prose

That rains fire on those

Whose roses are closed

An internal warrior

ON THE OUTSIDE LOOKING IN

Fights fear with fear

Anger with anger; yet never shedding a tear

Never showing blood, for his blood his clear

He approaches the sector, of his boss so dear

And engulfs him with pride, for fear conquers mere

I am an internal warrior

Vanquishing all emotional spears

Jesus via Luke

I push myself eight days a week

To be the best that I can be

À la Atlas, I lift the entire world above me

But alas, upon me falls the debris of the world crumbling

I feel such indescribable pain, inside of my brain

I pray every day for this anguish to escape

À la Jesus via Luke; hear what he has to say

Is what I'm told, but I can't; the pain is eating me away

I cannot sit perfectly still, and just relax

My legs are dead; the black is about to attack

A la Rumpelstiltskin; soon enough my legs will
detach

Cut off from my thoughts, a literality so sad

Missing: Title

I'm not going to keep playing this game

You're my puzzle piece just because of the fact that I am lame

The pain is coming at me like a fucking train

You're tying me to the tracks, but I can't complain

ON THE OUTSIDE LOOKING IN

RUSSELL LEHMANN

2012

RUSSELL LEHMANN

The Premature Burial

He was a man of mighty words

He was loved throughout the town!

He preached to the needy herds

When in their sorrows they drowned

He was a man of many years

But his soul was so young!

Yet he could not help but fear

That his time here on earth was about done

He was a man in fast decline

His physical essence was about gone!

The crowds waited in line

To declare their "so longs"

RUSSELL LEHMANN

He was a man now passed on

For his body was so cold!

Yet his soul stayed strong

And never left its mold

He was a man now entombed

For the grief was so strong!

There was a feeling of disquietude

As he was lowered under the lawn

He was a man who was now resting

In such a pleasant peace!

The people put forth their blessings

To the disappointment of his soul, for it was not yet deceased!

He was a man all alone

Now all alone in the ground!

Yet unfeasibly he uttered a moan

ON THE OUTSIDE LOOKING IN

While his eyes looked around

He was a man now alive

Brought back from the dead!

Hi soul had survived

Helping to keep his heart fresh

He was a man stricken with luck

Yet in unison with misfortune!

For he was now forever stuck

In a box of retention!

He was a man now hoping to be saved

But he had to come to terms!

His future had fatefully been paved

For death was quickly approaching with yearn!

RUSSELL LEHMANN

What is Poetry?

Poetry is the sound of a hummingbird's wings

Flapping through the air

As it sets out to feed

Poetry is that special night

When you wish upon a star

Hoping that all will be right

Poetry is the hot sand beneath one's feet

On a hot summer day

While frolicking on the beach

Poetry is the love that is emitted from the heart

When two people come together

ON THE OUTSIDE LOOKING IN

Vowing never to be torn apart

Poetry is the wherewithal to slam on the brakes

When a child darts across the street

Oblivious to his surroundings when he plays

Poetry is the ecstasy that fills your mood

As your taste buds rejoice with pleasure

When you eat your favorite food

Poetry is that wandering shadow

That follows you around

In your everyday travels

Poetry is a dancing flame

That brightens the room

During thunder and rain

Poetry is the rising steam

That escapes from a mug

Filled with coffee or tea

Poetry is the warmth upon your face

On a hot summer morning

When you retrieve the news of the day

Poetry is that special feeling

When you help someone cross the street

When their body is unwilling

Poetry is the glimmer of Lady Liberty

As immigrants would approach the shores

Of the country where dreams are possibilities

Poetry is the sound of cries

As a newborn baby

Looks his mom in the eyes

ON THE OUTSIDE LOOKING IN

Poetry is the anguish of death

When mourners gather to remember a loved one

After the soul from its body has left

Poetry is the line of baby ducks

Who follow their mother

And in whose love they trust

Poetry is the sound of a tree

Falling in a deep, dark forest

With no one around to hear or see

Poetry is the blood from Sierra Leone

That is shed upon diamonds

By fathers who are forced to leave their kids alone

Poetry is the paintings in the caves of Lascaux

So amazing, modern, articulate

Yet from 17,000 years ago

Poetry is the smell of a freshly cut lawn

On a hot summer day

That the sun had brought on

Poetry is whatever you want it to be

Whether you are feeling down

Or exuberant and happy

Wasting Away

I'm wasting away

Like a scarecrow losing its hay

Like a ghost ship off the bay

Like a rose left to decay

My soul has deteriorated

My personality is no more

My sense of humor is gone

And my smile, withered and worn

Sit me out on the curb, right next to the trash

To be picked up and taken away

My life is falling to pieces

So tie me up, so I don't blow away

RUSSELL LEHMANN

Be sure to look for the scar

On my left thumb, and you surely will

Uncover my crumbling body

As you traipse the depths of the glum landfill

But I urge you not to come looking for me

As for you there is nothing to gain

I urge you not to remember me

For the memories will be in vain

The Lost Jewels of King John[2]

It was mid-October in the year 1216

When misfortune had struck such a detested king

Lady luck was not fond of this royal man

For this king was to lose all that was grand

 A desperate journey was cut short due to sickness

For the king had fallen ill, and indeed this was witnessed

He was forced by his carriers to turn back at once

And the path they took, was taken by hunch

Now this king had brought with him

The crown jewels of the kingdom

And set about returning home

By a route soon to become bemoaned

By way of the Wash

They attempted to cross

Marshes and mud flats

In which they couldn't turn back

The King made it safely

But the crown jewels, you see,

Were capsized along with their wagon and horse

Into the marshes so thick, they could not continue
their course

Before long the king died

Due to illness and loss of pride

For the crown jewels were forever lost

And to this day are being sought

2In October of 1216, King John of England traveled to King's
Lynn in Norfolk. During the journey there, he fell ill with
dysentery and was forced to turn back. He had brought along

with him the crown jewels of England, and in the process of returning home, they were lost in the marshes of the Wash. To this day they have not been found.

The End

*"...I poured my heart out to you, let down my
guard swear to God*

*I'll blow my brains in your lap, lay here and die in
your arms*

*Drop to my knees and I'm pleading trying to stop
you from leaving..."*

~ Eminem, Space Bound

I am a shell of myself

So depressed deep down inside

I think I need some help

Never mind; just let me die

She walked away from me

Without ever saying goodbye

ON THE OUTSIDE LOOKING IN

She stole my heart's key

And threw it to the side

If I can't have her, no one can

I'll kill her with one shot

There's no amount of blood that I can't stand

I'll blow her f-ckin' brains up to the gods

Then I'll turn the gun on myself

And stick it straight under my chin

My body falling right next to where hers fell

And then our life together can begin

The 23rd of May

I did not cry today; my cheeks are dry today

For today was your birthday, and throughout the day I prayed

While I still wish you were here, I know in Heaven you get to play

Unlike here on earth, for so busy were the days

I can feel your spirit, swimming through my blood

And it comforts me to know that you're looking down from above

Your presence here on earth, I cannot explain how much I loved

I can feel you in my heart; your love comes rushing through in floods

I wish I had you back, but I know that you're still around

ON THE OUTSIDE LOOKING IN

Keeping watch over me as I have my ups and downs

We had, and still do, have a relationship so tightly bound

You will never leave my side, for this I have now found

So I wish you a happy birthday

For it celebrates the way

That you made me who I am today

And in you, I will ALWAYS have faith

That I Am, That I Am

I am a lonely and desperate man

That I am, that I am

My days are as banal

As the rooster's morning crow

Cock-a-doodle…you guessed it

At night I dream of having friends

Euphoria is infused into the heart of my heart

I wake up to my daily nightmare: that it was all
pretend

I only laugh for the sake of practicing my laugh

In case I ever need it, in case I ever need it

Will I ever need it?

ON THE OUTSIDE LOOKING IN

Dates are like drugs, drugs are like dates

I get a taste of the outside world, then POOF!

Once I finish walking her to her car, I crash from the high

Can I call her the next morning?!

No, I must adhere to society's rules

Hell no! Society can read between the lines of my index and ring fingers

I'm calling her, I'm calling her right now!

My lips tremble with fear as I listen to the dreadful tune of endless rings

No answer…I leave a message…I wait for a call back, which I know will never come

I check my phone every five minutes, every two minutes, every 30 seconds

Still no response, but I already knew this would happen, why am I surprised?

I think I'll stop dating

RUSSELL LEHMANN

I will forever be alone and forlorn

For I am a lonely and desperate man

That I am, that I am

Oh, to Be a Bird

Oh, to be a bird, so weightless in the sky

Oh, to be a bird, for not a day does pass by

Oh, to be a bird, for it lives not a lie

Oh, to be a bird, that shall be my next life!

Abusive Me

I don't eat, I won't play, I can't even stay awake

I beat myself up every second of every day

I weep for hours, for it's too much to take

Six feet deep is the place where I would like to stay

Everyone tells me, that I need to leave my home

My partial alacrity soon turns into moans

I am scared of the perfidy that upon me may be bestowed

I need help in the highest degree, in order to re-gain my soul

My Demons

The imps, the demons, they all live in Hell!

Alas! I live there too; their presence I seek to quell

Their actions exhaust me mentally; they exploit all my vulnerabilities

When they are unmindful, I step on coals to reach their nests

I tread so very vigilantly, for one sound could disturb their rest

I must strive to conquer every last one, for to my happiness they hold the key

Straight from The Inferno, they haunt me in my sleep

They intrude upon my only thoughts that I deem fit to keep

Help me Lord! For I am in frantic need of guidance from your heart!

RUSSELL LEHMANN

These creatures live to prey on me

They deprive me of my solemn liberties

Help me Lord! For they are on the doorstep of tear-
ing my life apart!

They pierce my soul with tridents

The pain leaves me seeking guidance

Yet I am in this fight alone; Hell is nothing more
than a void of anguish

How to win this fight I do not know

I try and try, but all is woe

Still I will fight with all my heart, until death be-
comes my only wish

When in doubt, I try to run

The imps and demons think it fun

They chase me until I fall into the cavernous pits
of fire

I start to melt

I cry for help

ON THE OUTSIDE LOOKING IN

As the wicked fiends laugh and play their lyres

Hell is becoming hotter

My self-assurance has been slaughtered

I search within myself to find that I'm too weak to carry on

My mind has been in so much pain

I ponder stopping this fight, for it has been in vain

I pray to the Lord to help me endure, and for these evil beings to be gone

I will always reside in this cavern of flames

Yet I have no complaints, there is no one to blame

I hope soon that my failures will help me brew a potent vigor

That will defeat these doers of iniquity

That will crush their actions of pure immorality

And help me to live a life in which I defend my thoughts with forceful rigor

Life Without a Head

Life without a head

How amazing that would be!

Your heart would be to hear,

While your soul would be to see!

Life without a head

What a shift of destiny!

No nose or mouth be needed,

For what would be the need to breathe?

Life without a head

How all stress would be set free!

Free from all daily troubles,

Oh, what a philosophy!

Life without a head

ON THE OUTSIDE LOOKING IN

No more pain of a brain that bleeds!
No more burns from a hellish life,
Such a delight in the life of me!

Life without a head
How easy that would be!
Confirm this with Mr. Crane,
For he knows not what agony means!

Life without a head
Oh, how can I make this be?!
Longing for a life that's blissful,
This life I begin to foresee

Life without a head
A fantasy that cannot be,
With my soul to see, and my heart to hear,
I shall journey towards a life of glee!

RUSSELL LEHMANN

I Hope that You Stay

You must understand that I've had no friends since the day that I was 12

I've had nothing to do but to just sit at home and into my thoughts just delve

So pardon me if I am coming on too strong, for I am truly a desperate man

The feeling I get when holding your hand is one you will never comprehend

I'm infatuated with you, I'm obsessed with you, and I'm taken by you in every single way

You've given me the friendship that I have always dreamed of, and I'll do anything to make you stay

I'm paranoid that you will leave me, trying to find meaning behind your every little move

I go insane when you're not with me; I tear my hair out when I'm not with you

ON THE OUTSIDE LOOKING IN

I need you by my side every second of every day,
the feelings I have for you are so strong

Yet I still don't truly know how you feel about me,
and I hope my underlying thoughts are wrong

I'm not a patient man when it comes to this game,
for I've been hurt too many times before

I want to be with you, and I hope you feel the
same, but if not then let the rain just pour

We haven't seen each other in so many days, and
to be honest I feel like slicing my throat

My head hurts so much I could reach for the gun,
without even bothering to leave a note

Tears stream down my cheeks as I sit at home,
thinking of all the good times that we've shared

I anxiously await seeing your beautiful face, your
gorgeous smile and your exceptional hair

So let the truth be known that I'm falling for you,
or at least that I think I am

For I have never held these feelings before, and I
am truly your biggest fan

I pray to God every night that everything will turn

out how I wish it to be

You are the most magnificent woman, and I hope
that our destiny is that we are meant to be

Enough

Synapses, neurons, are vital to life

But these crucial facets are detrimental to mine

Ablaze all the time with thoughts that bind

My mind to the chair, with the sponge wet and primed

An explosion of thoughts, a cacophony of sorts

Render me helpless, as I crumble once more

Expletives are shouted to these notions I abhor

But they only grow stronger, for winds make the fire roar

These unrelenting ideas have started to persuade

My once innocent mind to believe what they say

I used to fight back, but now I just lay

And accept the torment that I have come to obey

I've waved the white flag, I have no more strength to persevere

I'll go down with this ship, the water feels so sincere

I look down from this cliff, into the abyss I do not fear

For when I take this last step, my mind will be cleared

Corvus frugilegus

I have always loved animals

And they've loved me back

My tender caresses

Make them instantly attached

The finest of animals

Would have to be birds

Wild birds, in fact,

For their beauty need not words

For several years I have observed

All types of avian

Enthusiastically watching them

Glide with the wind

I even feed the pests

Crows, rooks and pigeons

Tossing bread left and right

As they follow me in legions

But one day occurred

Such an unfortunate deed

When a rook nipped my finger

While I was feeding it seed

How mad I became!

I wondered just why

I wanted to strike the bird

And watch it drop before my eyes!

An urge of such hatred!

To see it writhe would be nice,

To hear it caw with such pain

ON THE OUTSIDE LOOKING IN

As it gives up its fight

Sagacious I was

For I clenched the rooks throat

This brought me the joy

That I had such eagerly hoped!

As the rook grew weaker

He cawed one last cry

I felt such a release

As it finally died

After such an utter rush,

My vision soon left

My sense went numb

As I started to sweat

I soon found myself

Jumping out of my bed

Disgusted by my dream

Until I remembered what I had read

Just before I drifted off,

I read a short story by Poe

Which must have induced a phantasm

For it indeed induced woe

A story of such evil

And of delirious acts

For I feel you must be informed

If you are to read "The Black Cat"

Bring Me Death

"And then there stole into my fancy, like a rich musical note, the thought of what sweet rest there must be in the grave." ~ Edgar Allan Poe's

"The Pit and the Pendulum"

I cut myself yesterday for the very first time

No blood was drawn, much to my dislike

I should have cut deeper, for what's the point of life?

It's filled with nothing but pain, and nothing but strife

I kept imagining myself sticking a gun into my mouth

And pulling the trigger, brains spewing about

At this time, my will to survive was nothing to tout

For I wanted to end it all, which my strength wouldn't allow

Nothing in my life goes right, and that's not a self-defeating thought

It's the truth; I am cursed and always will be, until the day I fall into my plot

I'd be much happier if I was dead, for onto me no pain could be brought

I've lost every battle, every fight that I've fought

So at the end of this poem, don't be surprised if I'm dead

Don't be surprised to see me with a bullet in my head

Don't be surprised to see me hanging from the tree by the shed

Don't be surprised if you see me, relieved from all the dread

Angela

I've had many people in my life

But no one quite like you

With your persona that makes me naturally high

And your brown eyes of an incredible hue

I make it through the most depressing days

By just imagining your sweet, white smile

You make my problems phase away

And make me giggle like a child

How I stumbled upon you, I will never know

For you are as perfect as perfect can be

Your radiance of beauty emits an everlasting glow

A glow that even Venus could not beat

You're not even worth comparing to any other
woman around

For your essence will truly never be matched

You walk with such passion, as your feet grace the
ground

While you stand with such splendor that will for-
ever last

You've turned my life right-side up

A feat that no one has ever accomplished

For before I met you, my life was so rough

You are the angel that fulfilled my wish

You are so very young, yet mature beyond the years

Your self-determination is nothing less than out-
standing

You are not afraid to confront your fears

And your passion for life becomes ever more charm-
ing

There is a reason your name means angelic

For surely angels had a hand in your creation

ON THE OUTSIDE LOOKING IN

Your soul should be forever treasured as a relic

While your heart deserves the most prolonged ovation

So let it be known that you are second to none

You are the epitome of any man's dream

You deserve the best, for you are number one

No woman will ever come close to your sheen

A Tune of Truth

As my ears grasp the sounds of this song

It reminds me of the times that were spent with you

But would you know that I hate this song?

And I despise the thoughts of you

So slow is the tempo, at which this song plays

Much like yourself, for you hated to learn

Your lack of knowledge put me into such a frenzy of a craze

The lowest diploma of studies, you did not even yearn to earn

The lyrics of this song are at all times banal

Like the effect on your face, as you uttered your words

ON THE OUTSIDE LOOKING IN

The physiognomy of your movements, sparked within me such gall

I pretended to like you, which ultimately made me want to purge

A song of such romance, and of considerable love

Opposed the feeling of our kiss, for it was as dull as could be

You wanted to be close, so you gave me a hug

It was like embracing a corpse, for I wanted to flee

Thankfully, this song is about to come to its end

Like when you left me for an ignorant, arrogant abuser

I thanked God when you left, for I no longer needed to pretend

I was free from your slow wits; I was free from a loser

A Furious Sorrow

When I become depressed

I become increasingly angry

Rage boils inside me until I can't compress

The violent thoughts that transform me

Is it a shame or is it factual

That these feelings shouldn't be felt?

For I believe that they are natural

When such a hand has been dealt

Thinking about taking action

On these thoughts is surely wrong

But pondering them is a normal reaction

Just never make them a reality; sit still and be strong

ON THE OUTSIDE LOOKING IN

I apologize with much sorrow

To bring you into my thoughts

But I think you should know

What my anger makes me think about a lot

I think about the one person I truly hate, for he messed up my life

I picture sticking a gun down his throat and blowing him to pieces

I imagine kicking his dead body with all of my might

These are the gruesome thoughts that my anger releases

I continue on to think about slicing his throat

Eventually decapitating him, while stabbing his body non-stop

I'd take a gun to his lone head, the walls with blood I would coat

Then throw him out a ten-story window and rejoice as he dropped

I cannot change what I feel

I cannot change what I think

But these thoughts help me heal

They help me step away from the brink

Thoughts are just thoughts, nothing more, nothing less

They only become an issue when you make them a reality

So I put my violent thoughts onto paper to express

The ferocious anger within me, to thwart them from actuality

So don't be afraid if you ever think such fierce thoughts

For they are a natural way of coping when you're in doubt

Just let them flow through your mind and eventually they'll stop

Just know to never give in to them and to never act them out

A Better Man

"You question him yourself: he tells you he is in love, or unhappy, it is the same thing. And is anybody unhappy about another, unless they are in love with them?"

~ Horace Walpole's "Castle of Otranto"

I was falling for you

Yet I did not love you

You left too soon

For my feelings to bloom

You were my Annabel Lee

You were all I could see

You were too good to believe

You were the best thing that happened to me

I cherish all the memories

That we created with such hilarity

It did not seem like reality

For together we ended all our miseries

You resembled Beatrice, as I resembled Dante

For I was taken with you from the very first day

You captured my heart but then walked away

Metaphorically you died, but my feelings haven't strayed

The first time we kissed, was such a special night

As the stars shone above, emanating such a magical light

I never knew feelings could become such a blight

I was infected by you with adoring thoughts of such might

The two days we spent in The Paris of the West[3]

Were by far the best in my life, no less

Even though there were events that caused some stress

ON THE OUTSIDE LOOKING IN

The fun that we had overshadowed the rest

My life once again became empty
The moment that you left me
You tried to let my heart down easy
But all it did was bleed profusely

I hoped to be together
For more than forever
I did not care whether
This was a hopeless endeavor

I still don't know why you left
For you never took the breath
To explain to me in-depth
Your heart taking theft

I looked upon myself as the beast, and you as Belle

For you knew better than well not to dwell on the tale

The tale that has repelled many and has labeled me to no avail

You never did judge me, and with this you broke the spell

I can't stop thinking about you, you meant every-thing to me

I hate going to sleep, for you are in all my dreams

I try not to think about you, the pain causes me to do nothing but scream

I feel so dead inside, so let the requiem proceed

You haven't returned my many calls, I feel rejected to the highest

You didn't respond to my heartfelt letter, I redis-covered what to cry is

I thought you were mature, but these last few weeks have shown what your true side is

You gave my world such brightness, but now I'm just in one big crisis

ON THE OUTSIDE LOOKING IN

I'm starting to move on, even though I still want to
be friends

You told me you felt the same, but now I know that
was pretend

You ripped my heart out and tossed it in the trash,
but I know now that in the end

You gave me the experience I needed to become
an even better man

3San Francisco

And Again

It has been another year since the day you died

But for the first time I have yet to cry

Even though my soul still sinks in despair

I count you in my blessings, as if you were still here

When I delve into the thoughts of your life

I become immersed in flames of sorrow so rife

I douse myself in the rains of grief

Knowing that my pain will never be relieved

I've been having dreams of you lately

Which I've enjoyed immensely

Yet when I wake up it feels like déjà vu

For again it feels as if you died too soon

ON THE OUTSIDE LOOKING IN

It will probably be one year from now

That I write another poem about you and how

You affected my life in the most magnificent ways

And I know that in my heart, you will always be
there to stay.

RUSSELL LEHMANN

Klonopin

I'm feeling sick again

I need a Klonopin

What type of mess would that begin?

What type of mess would I be in?

This fight I cannot win

Unless I take a Klonopin

Voices are speaking out again

I cannot help but let them in

I throw caution to the wind

When I take these Klonopin

When will this habit end?

If my life's not on the mend

ON THE OUTSIDE LOOKING IN

I'm freaking out again

Where are my Klonopin?

I wish this was pretend

Mirrors look at me with such chagrin

Rehab is on the fringe

I need more Klonopin

The sunny days are getting dim

Why does my smile look so grim?

Within death I've come an inch

From my cravings of Klonopin

The thoughts of ending popping make me cringe

If it ends, I'll reach for the syringe

I've been a disgrace now ever since

I became glued to Klonopin

It has to be in my system

If my life is to not end

RUSSELL LEHMANN

I've rendered submission

To this vengeful Klonopin

When I try to stop popping them

Upon me falls a cataclysm

I'm at the point of exhaustion

My overuse of Klonopin

Now has me at wit's end

I need to get my life on track again

A hospital is not an option

For my separation from Klonopin

I'll use God to help me win

And conquer this addiction

So now I will begin

To wean away from Klonopin

And with the help of kith and kin

ON THE OUTSIDE LOOKING IN

I'll throw my last bottle in the bin-

With a Smile!

RUSSELL LEHMANN

Hallux Rigidus: A Poem of Literality

My toe destroyed my biggest dream

Which was the fame and fortunes of an athlete

It put on hold the plans I had for me

And continues to toy with my self-esteem

I was headed for a scholarship,

Until the cartilage in my toe was lost

The bones started to rub together

But I was determined to still play at all costs

Every step was bone-on-bone

The pain was unimaginably harsh

But I still led my team in sacks

ON THE OUTSIDE LOOKING IN

All because of the strength of my heart

After every practice, game, after everything, really,

I hopped away on just one foot

For the pain that I thought was unimaginably harsh

Surpassed the definition of hurt

After the season, and with no offers to play

I had a cheilectomy performed on my toe

The bones were shaved down, and many spurs re-
moved

The doctors were shocked by how I was able to
play my sport

After four months of recovery, I was back on track

My athletic abilities were as good as ever

I was able to dunk without any pain

And I thanked God that the anguish was over

I was professionally training for college football

In which I had made such mighty gains

Until right before the start of the season

When my toe was reintroduced with pain

The little cartilage I had remaining

Had now completely corroded

The spurs grew back in abundance

And the bones fiercely smashed together, erod-
ed

Back to the operating table I went

My mind and body in such despair

I had become accustomed to bad luck always
being by my side

But this was just too much to bear

My bones were shaved down to such an ab-
surdly size

While the spurs were once again removed

All the hope that I had left

ON THE OUTSIDE LOOKING IN

I had put into recovering for good

The doctor said it would be three months

Before I could return to my intense training

But I was never able to train again

For after six months the bones had not yet been healing

Eight months have now passed,

And the pain has once again returned

Fewer and fewer activities I can do

I'm headed for another surgery, which is to be my third

The one thing in my life that eliminates my stress

Has itself become eliminated

For I cannot even jog on beautiful summer days

Without a world of intense pain being created

I could say that I hate my life, but this is the

hand that I've been dealt

What are the odds of having three surgeries on a toe, especially at my age?

Such feelings of such intense rage I have felt

I have come to conclude that God's sole purpose, is just to play hateful games

ON THE OUTSIDE LOOKING IN

RUSSELL LEHMANN

2013

RUSSELL LEHMANN

Spoken Word

Dear Russell,

You're gonna go through some shit in your life.

You're gonna go through some real tough shit in your life.

I know you're just a young boy now, but I wanna speak up and warn you of what's about to go down.

Pretty soon, you're gonna lose all your friends

Pretty soon, you're gonna see life through a different lens

This probably doesn't even make sense,

But pretty soon you're gonna go insane…and wish you were dead.

I know you're really popular now, but pretty soon you're gonna be laughed at by other kids who won't know how,

You became such a pathetic wimp who was scared

to leave his own house

Who was scared to be in a crowd

Who thought a freaking whisper was so loud!

But listen, you will NEVER be a wimp, you will never be weak

You'll grow up to be stronger than a million ancient gods of Greece.

There are gonna be nights where you just stay up and cry

There are gonna be nights where you contemplate suicide

There are gonna be nights where you just wanna die

But you will have too much pride, to give up on your life

You're gonna be admitted to the psych ward three times

Where you'll see naked people trying to find walls to climb

ON THE OUTSIDE LOOKING IN

You're gonna be rushed to the ER way too much

But these experiences are the reason you're gonna grow up to be so tough

You're gonna have your dreams come crashing down

Just because some pathetic adult didn't want you around

You're gonna have your heart break as if it were made of glass

And have no friends to fall back on when the love of your life packs up her bags

You're gonna wish you were normal just like everybody else

But I need you to remember that you have a very bright future, even though you're gonna go through hell

Russell, I need you to be prepared for all the obstacles you're going to face

And at times you're gonna feel like you're trapped in a maze

And at times you're gonna feel like you've been so debased

And at times you're gonna go into a craze, and curse at the gods for why they made you this way!

But, Russell…I need you to listen to me.

You're not different now, but you will be.

Your life is going to be an utter disaster at times.

But within you is the strength you need to succeed

At being the best possible human being you can be.

So keep your chin up and keep your eyes on the prize.

Because we'll far surpass everyone's expectations of what we can accomplish in our life

But it won't be to your, or my, surprise.

Spoken Word--Unconquerable

When I was younger, I would get horrible images stuck in my head

Family members dead, their rotting corpses covered in the coagulated blood they bled

What was I to do?! I was a scared, no terrified, no PETRIFIED young boy, who just wanted these thoughts to be shed

My brain would hurt so much. The pain? Inconceivable. The good times? Irretrievable. These vile thoughts? Irrevocable! Or so it seemed...

You see, to me what seemed to be was only that which provoked misery, a cataclysmic hindrance to the society that is my well-being all the while thinking that what I was believing I was seeing. I would be seething when I would see these seemingly deceiving scenes, my head was teeming with these fleeting yet never relieving daydreams that were ever so repeating, and unperceiving was I being to their meaning.

RUSSELL LEHMANN

It was more than tough, seeing my mom, my dad, my sister lying dead before me. But I am SO MUCH stronger now. This? UNCONQUERABLE!

Spoken Word--Luck

What is Luck?

When it stands alone it is lost

Its worth stripped and tossed,

To the side like a cross

Thrown from the hand of an atheist raging with animos-

ity

Pity

Oh, what a pity

Its means mean no means

Unless it has a Good, or a Bad, with which it leads

Luck

It is nothing, just a figment of our self-deprecating

thoughts

But without it we are all lost

Like Luck itself,

When it stands alone

And at its mercy we will all pay

Its inevitable cost

Someone Else's Dream

I held her in my arms, in disbelief of where I was

I saw my reflection in her eyes, the expression on my face was love

I felt like I was dreaming, a reverie for the ages

Such a sentiment of cultured magic, apropos to the mages and sages

I asked a dollar for her thoughts, for their worth by far exceeds a penny

And she posed a question unheard of by me, and, boy, of these she has many

"What if this is only a dream? What if this isn't even real?"

My body shuddered in defiance against this fatalistic appeal

I replied, "If that is so, I hope to forever be asleep"

She then gave me a look, I didn't comprehend her means

She said, "What if this is a dream, not our own, but someone else's?"

What if everything we know is fake, all the moments that leave us breathless?"

From this query I was left speechless, my mind was tangled in a web

As fantastical as this was, I worried the truth was where these thoughts led

Both of us were left silent, by this idea that was not easy to condone

At any second, we could both be gone, two figments of a dream not our own

I continued to hold her in my arms, hoping that what she posed couldn't really be true

And then I told her:

"Even if we cease to exist, and I never again lay my eyes on you

I do know one thing factual, and that is true love is always...true."

RUSSELL LEHMANN

It is Said…

It is said that the caged bird sings of freedom

But what does it know of this freedom? Has it traipsed through nature's kingdom?

Was it captured and caged on a fine summer evening, as it was enjoying the Garden of Eden?

Did it taste the red berries from the Yew tree in season?

It is said that the caged bird sings of freedom

I ask myself, "For this, what could be the reason?"

Untitled Song

There aren't enough curse words to express my heart that broke

I'll fuckin slice you in the throat

Throw you in the middle of the road

Drive over you with my ford, Honda accord

And if I could afford it, I'd buy a John Deere and mow

Over your fuckin' face and do it some more

Don't think I'm done, bitch

RUSSELL LEHMANN

Bitter Feast

I've had my Annabel Lee, or so I thought

She brought angst to the table and fed me dis-
traught

Sweet

I went in not being sure as to what I was to find

But I found that diamond in the rough, a beautiful one of a kind

Her splendor could bring down the walls of Rome

While her radiance could light up the desert's night sky

Her smile could earn her a place on the throne

And her eyes can bring forth the truth from all lies

I didn't know what would come of us meeting

But now when she leaves my sight, she leaves my heart grieving

Her presence could defeat the most powerful of armies

Her aura could set flames to the most sodden of
plants

Her scent could attract the sweet swarm of honey
bees

While her body could melt the heart of any man

I went in not being sure as to what I was to find

But now every time I see her, she blows my mind

Aokigahara[1]

The dense forest lets little light in

Branches are chafed and scarred from ropes

The Sea of Trees drowns the people within

People who have lost everything; hope

Many who travel here will not travel home

Unless home to them is the shadow of death

Bodies hanging here, and over there lay the bones

Of those who came to draw their last breath

The forest of Aokigahara is destitute of brightness

For the trees do their best to block out the sun

One could say that these trees are full of shyness

Or perhaps ashamed of what their branches have done

These woods of bereavement will continue to house

Lifeless bodies that were once filled with pride

The doomed entrants will continue to allow

This once beautiful forest to be chided, despised

1Aokigahara is a 14-square-mile forest that lies at the north-west base of Mount Fuji in Japan. The forest contains a number of rocky, icy caverns, a few of which are popular tourist destinations. Due to the wind-blocking density of the trees and an absence of wildlife, the forest is known for being exceptionally quiet. The forest has a historic association with demons in Japanese mythology and is a popular place for suicides.

ON THE OUTSIDE LOOKING IN

RUSSELL LEHMANN

2017

RUSSELL LEHMANN

Just a Little

I want to kill myself, but I don't want to die
Yet I'm already dead inside, no longer alive

I resent this world, so I let it pass me by
I'm ashamed to be a part of this existential lie

My soul withers, my heart bleeds dry
My mind it screams, too angry to cry

I look up at the stars, my best friend is the sky
Yet it never answers my question of why

Maybe one day I'll find peace, just a little would suffice
In the meantime, however, I'll try my best to get by

RUSSELL LEHMANN

Tough

The toughest times do not last
But the toughest minds sure do

The darkest days always pass
You'll find this to be true

Cherish each moment, good or bad
They make you, well, you

Take them in, for they go by fast
So just enjoy the view

Bloody Mess

My mom is gone, I'm home alone
A necessity of the world's ways
For how long, I never really know
Minutes? Hours? Maybe days...

Hesitantly, she kissed me goodbye
Tears dropping from her face
Landing on my cheeks, once dry
As she gave me a lasting embrace

I sit in the corner, curled up in a ball
Biting my nails helps ease the stress
My mind compresses, as I start to bawl
And rip my fingers into a bloody mess

Anxiety pulsing through my veins

Depression leaking into my soul

OCD yearning to reign

Over a feeble boy, never whole

I need to move, to and fro

Or in circles, to sooth my pain

Motion seems to thwart a foe

Whose cackles echo throughout my brain

Boy to Man

I write these words with nothing to give
My heart, my soul, content to forfeit
I must indeed say, that it is too much to live
This life of mine, perhaps I'll quit

I give hope to others
Yet here I am, desperate
A broken man…
Maybe I'll quit

A bright light in the dark
That for too long has been lit
Perhaps it's time to disembark
On this venture deemed unfit

Should I quit?

Methinks it's time to rest

And merely relax for a bit

I've grown weary of giving my best

I must admit I may just quit

As I close my eyes, I hear a voice

Its crescendo akin to an orchestra pit

My eyelids raise to see a boy

Promising himself to never quit

Slowly down his cheeks tears flow

As he rises in bed to sit

The only thing he seems to know

Is that he will not quit

The boy looks at me, as I stare back at him

Timid, I do admit

ON THE OUTSIDE LOOKING IN

Mouth agape, I question him,

"Why not the urge to quit?"

"I know not much, but I possess the wit"

The boy says to me with stout spirit

"To follow my heart and dreams with grit

For to quit, I will not permit"

"I am you, and you are me

Surely you must see this." He continues his analy-
sis

I grow into you, and you blossom from me

To quit now would be amiss"

I continue to stare into my eyes

A brilliant gleam of trust they emit

An epiphany strikes, as I begin to cry

How could I have missed it?

I've given hope to myself all along

There is no reason that I should quit

Giving up would only prove myself wrong

I think I'll stick around for a bit

So I'm here to say that I'm here to stay,

This burden I carry I now see as a gift

My mission too vital, to further delay

How can I quit, when I was meant to uplift?

Reflection

There are nights I feel like running away

I have no home, no place to stay

I am not me; I deserve to be

Whatever I look into the mirror and see

I come and go, as I please

Into the depths of my mind, diseased

I'm just a man who struggles to be

The person he wishes the world to see

Rising

I've lost many battles but won many wars

Against these monsters that I abhor

Ripping up floorboards to search for more

Their sleeping snores, awakening to roars

No more can I ignore, my need to score

The blood of these demons, for I do indeed adore

The taste of victory; a fanatical matador

I have become, in my quest for triumph, evermore

Afraid before, now no more

From under the shadows I rise forth

Into the gleaming light, I soar

Rising from ashes, the phoenix of lore

Coffin Made to Fit

I dropped out of school

In 3rd, 4th and 5th

The last of which was the final nail

In a coffin made to fit

No longer in school

I was at home with myself

Where we would not play but fight

In the surreal realm of hell

I never learned to swim

In the tears I was drowning in

Rather I learned to give in

To an outlook so grim

Alive? Yes

Living? No

I was only existing

In the shadow of woe

I was young, too young

To understand death

But if I had, I can ensure

That I would have taken my last breath

Only sleep could combat

The torment of a living nightmare

My eyes would slowly close

As I would dream to forever disappear

ON
THE
OUTSIDE
LOOKING
IN

My life on the Autism Spectrum

Made in the USA
Middletown, DE
03 March 2022

62080475R00265